Oracle® PL/SQL

Training Guide

Ben Forta

BPB PUBLICATIONS
20 Ansari Road, Darya Ganj, New Delhi-110002

FIRST EDITION 2016

ISBN : 978-81-8333-451-8

Reprinted in India under arrangement with Pearson Education Inc., USA

Authorized reprint from the English language edition, entitled ORACLE PL/SQL IN 10 MINUTES, SAMS TEACH YOURSELF, 1st Edition, 9780672328664 by FORTA, BEN, published by Pearson Education, Inc, publishing as Sams Publishing, Copyright © 2016 Pearson Education, Inc.

Distributors:

COMPUTER BOOK CENTRE
12, Shrungar Shopping Centre,
M.G.Road, Bengaluru–560001
Ph: 25587923/25584641

MICRO BOOKS
Shanti Niketan Building,
8, Camac Street, Kolkata-700017
Ph: 22826518/22826519

DECCAN AGENCIES
4-3-329, Bank Street,
Hyderabad-500195
Ph: 24756967/24756400

MICRO MEDIA
Shop No. 5, Mahendra Chambers,
150 DN Rd. Next to Capital Cinema,
V.T. (C.S.T.) Station, Mumbai-400 001
Ph: 22078296/22078297

BPB BOOK CENTRE
376 Old Lajpat Rai Market,
Delhi-110006
Ph: 23861747

INFOTECH
G-2, Sidhartha Building,
96, Nehru Place,
New Delhi -110019
Ph: 41619735, 26438245

BPB PUBLICATIONS
20, Ansari Road, Darya Ganj
New Delhi-110002
Ph: 23254990/23254991

Published by Manish Jain for BPB Publications, 20, Ansari Road, Darya Ganj, New Delhi-110002 and Printed at Akash Press, New Delhi.

Contents

About the Author

Ben Forta has three decades of experience in the computer industry in product design and development, support, training, and marketing. As Adobe Inc.'s Senior Director of Education Initiatives, he spends a considerable amount of time teaching, talking, and writing about Adobe products, coding and application development, creativity, and digital literacy and provides feedback to help shape the future direction of Adobe products.

Ben is the author of more than 40 books, including the world's best-selling title on SQL, as well as titles on topics as diverse as Regular Expressions, mobile development, and Adobe ColdFusion. More than 750,000 copies of his books are in print in English, and titles have been translated into fifteen languages. Many of these titles are used as textbooks in colleges and universities worldwide.

Education is Ben's passion. Between writing, lecturing, and in-classroom experience, Ben has dedicated his professional and personal lives to teaching, inspiring, and sharing his love for technology and creativity. He is immensely grateful to have had the opportunity to share with millions worldwide.

Ben is also a successful entrepreneur with experience creating, building, and selling start-ups. He is a sought-after public speaker, a writer, and a blogger, and he presents on education and development topics worldwide.

Acknowledgments

It's been sixteen years since the publication of my first book on SQL, *Sams Teach Yourself SQL in 10 Minutes*. That book was met with such positive feedback that it has been updated three times, has spawned four spin-off titles (the most recent being the book you are reading right now), and has been translated more than a dozen times. In all of its various flavors and iterations, this little book has helped hundreds of thousands learn the basics of SQL. So, first and foremost, thanks to all of you who have trusted me and this book over the years; your support is both incredibly humbling and a source of great pride.

I am blessed with some very vocal and opinionated readers who regularly share ideas, comments, suggestions, and occasionally criticism. These books continue to improve directly in response to that feedback, so thanks, and please keep it coming.

Thanks to the numerous schools and colleges the world over who have made this series part of their curriculum. Seeing students use my writing as part of their studies never ceases to thrill.

And finally, thanks to my partners at Pearson with whom I've now published more than 40 titles, and without whose support none would have seen the light of day. In particular, thanks to Betsy Gratner for shepherding this book through the process, Paula Lowell for her editing help, and Mark Taber for once again patiently and encouragingly supporting whatever I toss his way.

Ben Forta

We Want to Hear from You!

As the reader of this book, *you* are our most important critic and commentator. We value your opinion and want to know what we're doing right, what we could do better, what areas you'd like to see us publish in, and any other words of wisdom you're willing to pass our way.

We welcome your comments. You can email or write to let us know what you did or didn't like about this book—as well as what we can do to make our books better.

Please note that we cannot help you with technical problems related to the topic of this book.

When you write, please be sure to include this book's title and author as well as your name and email address. We will carefully review your comments and share them with the author and editors who worked on the book.

Introduction

Oracle Database (or Oracle RDBMS) is so prevalent and well established that most users simple refer to it as "Oracle" (ignoring the fact that Oracle, the company, produces other software, and even hardware). Oracle Database (I'll do what most do and just call it "Oracle" to simplify things) has been around since the 1970s, making it one of the earliest database management systems. Oracle is one of the most used database management systems (DBMS) in the world. In fact, most surveys rank it as #1 in database use and popularity worldwide, especially among corporate users, and over the years it has proven itself to be a solid, reliable, fast, and trusted solution to all sorts of data storage needs.

That's the good news. The not-so-good news is that getting started with Oracle can be tricky, especially when compared to some of the alternative DBMSs. Oracle's power, capabilities, security, and more are an important part of why it is so trusted. But that makes installation, configuration, and even the tooling a little more complex, too. On top of that, Oracle's implementation of the SQL language, called PL/SQL, tends to differ subtly from other SQL implementations, and this can make using Oracle just a bit trickier.

What Is This Book?

This book is based on my best-selling *Sams Teach Yourself SQL in 10 Minutes*. That book has become one of the most used SQL tutorials in the world, with an emphasis on teaching what you really need to know—methodically, systematically, and simply. However, as popular and as successful as that book is, it does have some limitations:

- In covering all the major DBMSs, coverage of DBMS-specific features and functionality had to be kept to a minimum.
- To simplify the SQL taught, the lowest common denominator had to be found—SQL statements that would (as much as possible) work with all major DBMSs. This requirement necessitated that better DBMS-specific solutions not be covered.

- Although basic SQL tends to be rather portable between DBMSs, more advanced SQL most definitely is not. As such, that book could not cover advanced topics, such as triggers, cursors, stored procedures, access control, transactions, and more, in any real detail.

And that is where this book comes in. *Sams Teach Yourself Oracle PL/SQL in 10 Minutes* builds on the proven tutorials and structure of *Sams Teach Yourself SQL in Ten Minutes*, without getting bogged down with anything but Oracle and PL/SQL. Starting with simple data retrieval and working toward more complex topics, including the use of joins, subqueries, regular expressions, full text-based searches, stored procedures, cursors, triggers, table constraints, and much more. You'll learn what you need to know methodically, systematically, and simply—in highly focused lessons designed to make you immediately and effortlessly productive.

Who Is This Book For?

This book is for you if

- You are new to SQL.
- You are just getting started with Oracle PL/SQL and want to hit the ground running.
- You want to quickly learn how to get the most out of Oracle and PL/SQL.
- You want to learn how to use Oracle in your own application development.
- You want to be productive quickly and easily using Oracle without having to call someone for help.

It is worth noting that this book is not intended for all readers. If you are an experienced SQL user, then you might find the content in this book to be too elementary. However, if the preceding list describes you and your needs relative to Oracle, you'll find *Sams Teach Yourself Oracle PL/SQL in 10 Minutes* to be the fastest and easiest way to get up to speed with Oracle.

Companion Website

This book has a companion website at `forta.com/books/0672328666`. Visit the site to

- Access table creation and population scripts for creating the example tables used throughout this book
- Visit the online support forum
- Access online errata (if one might be required)
- Find other books that might be of interest to you

Conventions Used in This Book

This book uses different typefaces to differentiate between code and regular English, and also to help you identify important concepts.

Text that you type and text that should appear on your screen appears in `monospace` type. `It looks like this to mimic the way text looks on your screen.`

Placeholders for variables and expressions appear in *`monospace italic`* font. You should replace the placeholder with the specific value it represents.

This arrow (➥) at the beginning of a line of code means that a single line of code is too long to fit on the printed page. Continue typing all the characters after the ➥ as if they were part of the preceding line.

> NOTE
>
> A Note presents interesting pieces of information related to the surrounding discussion.

> TIP
>
> A Tip offers advice or teaches an easier way to do something.

CAUTION

A Caution advises you about potential problems and helps you steer clear of disaster.

New Term sidebars provide clear definitions of new, essential terms.

Input ▼

The Input icon identifies code that you can type in yourself. It usually appears by a listing.

Output ▼

The Output icon highlights the output produced by running Oracle PL/SQL code. It usually appears after a listing.

Analysis ▼

The Analysis icon alerts you to the author's line-by-line analysis of input or output.

LESSON 1

Understanding SQL

In this lesson, you'll learn about databases and SQL, prerequisites to learning about Oracle and PL/SQL.

Database Basics

The fact that you are reading this book indicates that you, somehow, need to interact with databases. And so before diving into Oracle and its implementation of the SQL language (PL/SQL), it is important that you understand some basic concepts about databases and database technologies.

Whether you are aware of it or not, you use databases all the time. Each time you select a name from your email or smartphone address book, you use a database. When you conduct a search on an Internet search site, you use a database. When you log in to your network at work, you validate your name and password against a database. Even when you use your ATM card at a cash machine, you use databases for PIN verification and balance checking.

But even though we all use databases all the time, much confusion remains about what exactly a database is. This is especially true because different people use the same database terms to mean different things. Therefore, a good place to start our study is with a list and explanation of the most important database terms.

> TIP: **Reviewing Basic Concepts**
>
> What follows is a brief overview of some basic database concepts. It is intended to either jolt your memory if you already have some database experience, or to provide you with the absolute basics if you are new to databases. Understanding databases is an important part of mastering Oracle, and you might want to find a good book on database fundamentals to brush up on the subject if needed.

What Is a Database?

The term *database* is used in many different ways, but for our purposes a database is a collection of data stored in some organized fashion. The simplest way to think of it is to imagine a database as a filing cabinet. The filing cabinet is simply a physical location to store data, regardless of what that data is or how it is organized.

> **Database** A container (usually a file or set of files) to store organized data.

> CAUTION: **Misuse Causes Confusion**
>
> People often use the term *database* to refer to the database software they are running. This is incorrect, and it is a source of much confusion. Database software is actually called the *Database Management System* (or DBMS). The database is the container created and manipulated via the DBMS. A database might be a file stored on a hard drive, but it might not. For the most part, this is not even significant because you never access a database directly anyway; you always use the DBMS and it accesses the database for you.

Tables

When you store information in your filing cabinet, you don't just toss it in a drawer. Rather, you create files within the filing cabinet, and then you file related data in specific files.

In the database world, that file is called a *table*. A table is a structured file that can store data of a specific type. A table might contain a list of customers, a product catalog, or any other list of information.

> **Table** A structured list of data of a specific type.

The key here is that the data stored in the table is one type of data or one list. You would never store a list of customers and a list of orders in the same database table. Doing so would make subsequent retrieval and access difficult. Rather, you would create two tables, one for each list.

Every table in a database has a name that identifies it. That name is always unique—meaning no other table in that database can have the same name.

> NOTE: **Table Names**
>
> What makes a table name unique is actually a combination of several things, including the database name and table name. This means that although you cannot use the same table name twice in the same database, you definitely can reuse table names in different databases.

Tables have characteristics and properties that define how data is stored in them. These include information about what data may be stored, how it is broken up, how individual pieces of information are named, and much more. This set of information that describes a table is known as a *schema*, and schema describe specific tables within a database, as well as entire databases (and the relationship between tables in them, if any).

> **Schema** Information about database and table layout and properties.

> NOTE: **Schema or Database?**
>
> Occasionally *schema* is used as a synonym for *database* (and *schemata* as a synonym for *databases*). While unfortunate, it is usually clear from the context which meaning of *schema* is intended. In this book, *schema* refers to the aforementioned definition.

Columns and Datatypes

Tables are made up of columns. A column contains a particular piece of information in a table.

> **Column** A single field in a table. All tables are made up of one or more columns.

The best way to understand a column is to envision database tables as grids, somewhat like spreadsheets. Each column in the grid contains a particular piece of information. In a customer table, for example, one column contains the customer number, another contains the customer name, and the address, city, state, and Zip Code are all stored in their own columns.

> TIP: **Breaking Up Data**
>
> It is extremely important to break data into multiple columns correctly. For example, city, state, and Zip Code should always be separate columns. By breaking these out, it becomes possible to sort or filter data by specific columns (for example, to find all customers in a particular state or in a particular city). If city and state are combined into one column, it would be extremely difficult to sort or filter by state.

Each column in a database has an associated datatype. A datatype defines what type of data the column can contain. For example, if the column is to contain a number (perhaps the number of items in an order), the datatype would be a numeric datatype. If the column were to contain dates, text, notes, currency amounts, and so on, the appropriate datatype would be used to specify this.

> **Datatype** A type of allowed data. Every table column has an associated datatype that restricts (or allows) specific data in that column.

Datatypes restrict the type of data that a column can store (for example, preventing the entry of alphabetical characters into a numeric field). Datatypes also help sort data correctly, and play an important role in optimizing disk usage. As such, you must give special attention to picking the right datatype when creating tables.

Rows

Data in a table is stored in rows; each record saved is stored in its own row. Again, envisioning a table as a spreadsheet style grid, the vertical columns in the grid are the table columns, and the horizontal rows are the table rows.

For example, a customer's table might store one customer per row. The number of rows in the table is the number of records in it.

> **Row** A record in a table.

> NOTE: **Records or Rows?**
> You might hear users refer to database *records* when referring to *rows*. For the most part, people use the two terms interchangeably, but *row* is technically the correct term.

Primary Keys

Every row in a table should have some column (or set of columns) that uniquely identifies it. A table containing customers might use a customer number column for this purpose, whereas a table containing orders might use the order ID. An employee list table might use an employee ID or the employee Social Security Number column.

> **Primary Key** A column (or set of columns) whose values uniquely identify every row in a table.

This column (or set of columns) that uniquely identifies each row in a table is called a *primary key*. You use the primary key to refer to a specific row. Without a primary key, updating or deleting specific rows in a table becomes extremely difficult because no guaranteed safe way exists to refer to just the rows to be affected.

> TIP: **Always Define Primary Keys**
> Although primary keys are not actually required, most database designers ensure that every table they create has a primary key so future data manipulation is possible and manageable.

You can establish any column in a table as the primary key, as long as it meets the following conditions:

- No two rows can have the same primary key value.
- Every row must have a primary key value (primary key columns may not allow NULL values).

> TIP: **Primary Key Rules**
>
> The rules listed here are enforced by Oracle itself.

You usually define primary keys on a single column in a table. But this is not required, and you may use multiple columns together as a primary key. When you use multiple columns, the rules previously listed must apply to all columns that make up the primary key, and the values of all columns together must be unique (individual columns need not have unique values).

> TIP: **Primary Key Best Practices**
>
> In addition to the rules that Oracle enforces, several universally accepted best practices that you should adhere to include the following:
>
> - Don't update values in primary key columns.
> - Don't reuse values in primary key columns.
> - Don't use values that might change in primary key columns. (For example, when you use a name as a primary key to identify a supplier, you would have to change the primary key when the supplier merges and changes its name.)

Another important type of key is the foreign key, but I'll get to that later on in Lesson 15, "Joining Tables."

What Is SQL?

SQL (pronounced as the letters *S-Q-L* or as *sequel*) is an abbreviation for Structured Query Language. SQL is a language designed specifically for communicating with databases.

Unlike other languages (spoken languages such as English, or programming languages such as C, Java, or Python), SQL is made up of very few words. This is deliberate. SQL is designed to do one thing and do it well—provide you with a simple and efficient way to read and write data from a database.

What are the advantages of SQL?

- SQL is not a proprietary language used by specific database vendors. Almost every major DBMS supports SQL, so learning this one language enables you to interact with just about every database you'll run into.
- SQL is easy to learn. The statements are all made up of descriptive English words, and there aren't that many of them.
- Despite its apparent simplicity, SQL is a very powerful language, and by cleverly using its language elements, you can perform complex and sophisticated database operations.

> NOTE: **DBMS-Specific SQL**
>
> Although SQL is not a proprietary language and a standards committee exists that tries to define SQL syntax that all DBMSs can use, the reality is that no two DBMSs implement SQL identically. The SQL taught in this book is specific to Oracle, and although much of the language taught is usable with other DBMSs, do not assume complete SQL syntax portability.

Try It Yourself

All the lessons in this book use working examples, showing you the SQL syntax, what it does, and explaining why it does it. I strongly suggest that you try each and every example for yourself to learn Oracle firsthand.

> NOTE: **You Need Oracle**
>
> Obviously, you'll need access to an Oracle DBMS to follow along. In Lesson 2, "Getting Started with Oracle and PL/SQL," I explain exactly what you need, and present several installation and configuration options that you can use.

Summary

In this first lesson, you learned what SQL is and why it is useful. Because SQL is used to interact with databases, you also reviewed some basic database terminology.

LESSON 2

Getting Started with Oracle and PL/SQL

In this lesson, you'll learn what Oracle and PL/SQL are, and what tools you can use to work with them.

What Is Oracle?

In the previous lesson, you learned about databases and SQL. As explained, it is the database software (*DBMS* or *Database Management System*) that actually does all the work of storing, retrieving, managing, and manipulating data. Oracle DBMS (or just "Oracle") is a DBMS; that is, it is database software.

Oracle has been around for a long time. The first version of the DBMS was released in the 1970s, and it has been updated and improved regularly ever since. The current (as of the time this book goes to print) version of Oracle is 12c, which was released in 2013 (the "c" in 12c stands for "cloud"). Oracle is one of the most deployed and used DBMSs, especially within corporate systems and infrastructures.

Client-Server Software

DBMSs fall into two categories: shared file–based and client-server. The former (which include products such as Microsoft Access and File Maker) are designed for desktop use, and are generally not intended for use on higher-end or more critical applications (including websites and web-based applications).

Databases such as Oracle, MySQL (and its offshoot MariaDB), and Microsoft SQL Server are client-server–based databases. Client-server applications are split into two distinct parts. The *server* portion is a piece of software that is responsible for all data access and manipulation. This software runs on a computer called the *database server.*

Only the server software interacts with the data files. All requests for data, data additions and deletions, and data updates are funneled through the server software. These requests or changes come from computers running client software. The *client* is the piece of software with which the user interacts. If you request an alphabetical list of products, for example, the client software submits that request over the network to the server software. The server software processes the request; filters, discards, and sorts data as necessary; and sends the results back to your client software.

> NOTE: **How Many Computers Do You Need?**
> The client and server software may be installed on two computers or on one computer. Regardless, the client software communicates with the server software for all database interaction, be it on the same machine or not.

All this action occurs transparently to you, the user. The fact that data is stored elsewhere or that a database server is even performing all this processing for you is hidden. You never need to access the data files directly. In fact, most networks are set up so that users have no access to the data, or even the drives on which it is stored.

Why is this significant? Because to work with Oracle, you need access to both a computer running the Oracle server software and client software with which to issue commands to Oracle:

- The server software is the Oracle DBMS. You can run a locally installed copy, or you can connect to a copy running a remote server to which you have access.
- The client can be Oracle-provided tools, scripting languages (such as Python and Perl), web application development languages (such as PHP, JSP, and ASP), programming languages (such as C, C++, and Java), and more.

> NOTE: **Clients? Servers? Why Should I Care?**
>
> The reason I point this out is that client-server software, by design, is a little more complex to get started with. When you use a word processor or spreadsheet, you open the application on your computer and it works with local data. Client-server database software doesn't work that way. Production servers usually run in data centers that users never access directly, so the computers running the server software seldom have client tools on them. Similarly, when working with these databases, users typically use local tools connected to remote production servers, so they would have client tools installed locally but not a server. As such, before those client tools can be used, they must be configured so that they can access the remote server. This is true even if both the server and client tools are indeed on the same machine, as you will see shortly.

PL/SQL

As I noted in Lesson 1, "Understanding SQL," all SQL implementations are *not* created equal. This is unfortunate; it would be ideal if you could learn and write SQL for one DBMS and have it run as-is on any other. In early SQL days, this was actually more likely, but over the years DBMS vendors have needed to add features and functionality beyond that supported by standard SQL, and so they created their own variants of the SQL language.

PL/SQL stands for *Procedural Language / Structured Query Language*, and PL/SQL is Oracle's implementation of SQL (and has been since Oracle version 7). The SQL you will learn in this book is PL/SQL, which means that it is intended for use with Oracle only. Most of what you'll learn, especially in the earlier lessons, is quite applicable to other DBMSs, but this definitely is not the case later in the book.

Client Tools

As already explained, Oracle is a client-server database, and to use it, you'll need client software (the program you use to actually run SQL commands). Lots of options exist in regard to client software, but you should be aware of these two Oracle options specifically:

- All Oracle server installations include a command-line tool called SQL*Plus. This basic client simply displays a `SQL>` prompt in a text window, allowing you to enter commands and instructions to the Oracle server.
- Oracle also provides a free graphical client called Oracle SQL Developer (it might show up named just "SQL Developer" when you install it on your computer). Oracle SQL Developer lets you interactively connect to and use your Oracle server and is a much better option for daily Oracle use, especially for beginners.

Although you are free to use any client tool you want (the PL/SQL you use will always be the same regardless of client tool), I highly recommend using Oracle SQL Developer as your first tool, and the instructions in this book assume that you are doing just that.

Getting Set Up

As you now know, to start using Oracle, and to follow along with the lessons in this book, you need access to an Oracle DBMS (or "Oracle Server") and client applications (software used to access the server).

What Software Do You Need?

You do not need your own installed Oracle server, but you do need access to one. You basically have two options:

- Access to an existing Oracle DBMS, perhaps one by your hosting company or place of business or school. To use this server, you will be granted a server account (a login name and password).
- You may download and install your own copy of Oracle for installation on your own computer. Oracle runs on major platforms including Windows and Linux, but no longer on Mac OS. However, that does not mean that Mac users can't learn and use Oracle PL/SQL.

NOTE: **Important Note for Mac Users**

Oracle has stopped officially supporting Mac OS as a server platform. If you are a Mac OS user, you can install the client software and use it to connect to a remote Oracle database server, but you won't be able to install the Oracle DBMS itself on your Mac (well, at least not easily or using any documented options). As such, Mac users must opt for the first of the two options noted previously.

TIP: **If You Can, Install a Local Server**

For complete control, including access to commands and features that you will probably not be granted by using someone else's Oracle DBMS, install your own local server. Even if you don't end up using your local server as your final production DBMS, you'll still benefit from having complete and unfettered access to all the server has to offer.

If you will be using an existing hosted Oracle server, then you don't need to worry about what version it is, because just about everything you'll learn in this book works with all versions (and if version-specific issues exist that you need to be aware of, I point them out along the way).

If you want to install your own server, then you have two choices:

- You can install a complete Oracle server installation. The current version (as of when this book is going to print) is Oracle 12c, and you can install that or any prior version. Oracle server is commercial software, and so although you can download and install it without buying a license, you need to purchase a license for ongoing use. When you install Oracle server, it presents you with lots (and I do mean lots) of configuration options that you can use to control exactly what gets installed and how it is configured.

- You can also download and install Oracle Database Express Edition (also called Oracle Database XE), a free version of Oracle server that has some important limitations, none of which will impact the lessons in this book. Installing Oracle Database Express Edition is quick and painless, and the PL/SQL you'll learn and use applies to all versions of Oracle server.

> TIP: **Oracle Database Express Edition Is Recommended**
>
> As should be apparent from the descriptions I just gave you, my recommendation is that if you are new to Oracle and want to focus on PL/SQL (as opposed to focusing on managing and administering an Oracle server), use the Express Edition. Installing and configuring a full-blown Oracle server can be frustrating if you've never done it before, and if your goal is to learn PL/SQL, that effort is unnecessary. The current (as of when this book is going to print) version of Oracle XE is 11g Release 2. However, if you truly do want to delve into the world of Oracle database administration, then by all means install the full Oracle DBMS.

Obtaining the Software

To learn more about Oracle, go to http://oracle.com/.

To download a copy of the server, go to the Oracle website and click on the Download link. Lots of options present themselves, but the ones that you are interested in are the following:

- In the Database section, select Oracle Database for a full Oracle server installation, or the Express Edition.
- In the Developer Tools section, select SQL Developer for the client tool.

Oracle does require the creation of an Oracle account to download any software, so if you don't have an existing account, the site prompts you to create one.

> NOTE: **Where Is Oracle SQL Developer?**
>
> Unlike SQL*Plus (which is always installed with Oracle server installations), you might need to install Oracle SQL Developer separately, depending on the version of Oracle server you are using. As of Oracle 12c, Oracle SQL Developer is indeed installed as part of the server installation. However, if you are using an older version of Oracle, or Oracle Express, you must download and install Oracle SQL Developer yourself.

Installing the Software

If you are installing a local Oracle server, do so before installing any other clients or utilities.

Exact installation steps for a full Oracle server are beyond the scope of this book, and if you need help with an installation, you should refer to documentation on the Oracle website.

Installation of Oracle Express Edition involves the following:

- Depending on your operating system, you might need to expand the download file to uncompress it.
- Run the setup program.
- Accept the license agreement.
- You can leave all questions and prompts with their default values.
- The programs asks you to provide a database password; enter one and remember what it is!
- Then just let the installer do its thing.

Regardless of whether or not you install a local server, you'll want a local copy of Oracle SQL Developer. If one was not installed (if and) when you installed the Oracle server, do the following:

- Depending on your operating system, you might need to expand the download file to uncompress it.

- Run the setup program.
- Accept the license agreement.
- You can leave all questions and prompts with their default values.
- Then just let the installer do its thing.

As long as the software installs correctly, you're ready to move on to Lesson 3, "Working with Oracle."

Summary

You now know what Oracle is, what PL/SQL is, and what software you need to proceed. You should also have access to an Oracle server (local or remote), and have client software installed and ready to use. In Lesson 3, I'll show you how to log in and log out of the server, and how to execute commands. The lessons in this book all use real SQL statements and real data, and so I will also walk you through creating and populating the example database tables.

LESSON 3

Working with Oracle

In this lesson, you learn how to connect and log in to Oracle, how to issue PL/SQL SQL statements, and how to create and populate the example tables that we'll be using throughout this book.

Creating a Working Environment

Now that you have access to Oracle and client software to use with it, the next step is to create a working environment. Database servers, like your Oracle server, are usually used by lots of different users and applications. Imagine what would happen if a user created a table called `customers` to store customer data, and another user tried to create a table of the same name. Users could overwrite each other's data; they could access incorrect information—you get the idea. In multi-user environments, and DBMSs are designed to be exactly that, this type of contention is a real concern. And so when working in client-server databases, it's important for each user to have a private safe workspace. Back to our example, by having this workspace, one user's `customers` table doesn't interfere with another user's table of the same name.

Many different ways exist to create safe, isolated work environments. If you are using an existing Oracle server, perhaps a corporate database, then the database administrator will likely give you your own login and workspace, and when you log in to Oracle, you'll be in the right safe workspace automatically. If this is the case, you can jump ahead to the later section, "Making the Connection."

If, however, you are using your own Oracle server, then you'll need to do this for yourself.

> CAUTION: **Not Required, But Highly Recommended**
>
> When Oracle is first installed, it creates one default instance. This is where Oracle itself stores system information, including user login details and more. The truth is that you can use this default system instance, too; you could create the example tables within it, populate them with the example data, and be able to proceed with the lessons in this book. However, using the default system instance for your own work is not recommended. In fact, doing so is generally considered a bad idea. Why? Well, as I just explained, this system instance is used to store information that Oracle DBMS itself needs, critical information without which the DBMS might not run properly (or maybe not run at all). As you will see in later lessons, editing data, even deleting entire tables, is all too easy to do, and so working and experimenting in the default system instance is asking for trouble. That's why I want you to create your own safe workspace, one other than the default system instance.

Creating a Dedicated Oracle Instance

The best way to create a safe work environment is to create a dedicated instance of Oracle for yourself. You can think of it as Oracle allowing multiple copies of itself to be run on a single server, each one isolated from another copy. Each server is referred to as an instance, and each instance has a unique name.

> NOTE: **Are You Using Oracle Express Edition?**
>
> The creation of multiple instances is supported by full Oracle installations only, but not by Oracle Express Edition. If you are using Express Edition, jump ahead to "Creating a Custom Workspace."

To create a dedicated Oracle instance for use with this book, do the following:

1. Run the Oracle installed application named Database Configuration Assistant; this is used to create (as well as update and delete) database instances.

2. When the application launches, select the first option, Create a Database, and then click the Next button.

3. You may be asked to select a Database Template. If so, select General Purpose and then click the Next button.

4. Every database must be uniquely named. In production environments, database names are carefully managed and are usually in the form `organization.domain.database`. However, to keep things simple, enter **`crashcourse`** as the Global Database Name and as the SID (the System Identifier), and then click the Next button.

5. If you are asked about Enterprise Manager, leave the default settings, and click the Next button.

6. You'll then be asked for passwords for important management accounts. You can enter a unique password for each account, or, as this is a non-mission-critical database instance, check the Use the Same Administrative Password option and provide a password. Remember this password; without it, you cannot access your new database instance. Click Next.

7. When asked about database storage locations and templates, leave the default settings, and click the Next button.

8. When asked about recovery options, once again, leave the default settings, and click the Next button.

9. Oracle can install sample tables and data in your new instance. We do not need this because we are going to use our own example data. So, when asked about Sample Schemas, make sure the box is not checked, and then click the Next button.

10. When asked about memory, sizing, character sets, and connections, leave the default settings, and click the Next button.

11. Eventually you'll be asked whether you want to create a database, create a database template, or generate database creation scripts. The only option you want checked is Create Database.

12. Click the Next button, and when prompted for confirmation, click the OK button.

The Oracle Database Configuration Assistant now creates your new `crashcourse` database instance.

> NOTE: **If You See Warning Messages**
>
> You might see warnings pertaining to specific settings. As long as the final screen says that the database instance creation completes successfully, you'll be good to go.

After your database instance has been created, you can jump to the later section, "Making the Connection."

Creating a Custom Workspace

If you are using Oracle Express Edition, you won't be able to create your own database instance. So instead, create a user-specific workspace within the existing database instance.

Here's what you need to do:

1. Oracle Express Edition is managed via an embedded web server. The Oracle Express Edition installer created a link named Get Started with Oracle Express Edition. Click the link, and a web browser opens displaying a web page with options to manage Storage, Sessions, and more. If you are prompted to log in, use the login name `SYSTEM` and the password you provided at installation time.
2. Click on the red Application Express button. You'll be presented with a web page that can be used to create an application workspace.
3. Make sure Create New is selected.
4. For Database Username, type **`crashcourse`**.
5. For Application Express Username, type **`crashcourse`** (or use your own name).
6. Enter a password of your choice and confirm it.
7. Click the red Create Workspace button.

8. You should see a prompt telling you that the workspace was successfully created, and allowing you to log in. Click on the login option. If you don't see the prompt, just click on the Application Express button again, and this time click on the Already have an account? Login Here button.

9. When prompted for Workspace, enter `crashcourse`; for Username, enter the username from step 5, and enter the Password you selected.

10. Click the *Login* button.

You should see a new screen with options for Application Builder, SQL Workshop, and more. If this is the case, you're ready to proceed.

> TIP: **You Can Use Application Express**
>
> Application Express is a web-based interface to Oracle Express Edition. Among its features is a tool named SQL Workshop that can be used to enter SQL statements, build scripts, and more. As such, Application Express is another Oracle client that you can use.

After your workspace has been created, you can jump to the following "Making the Connection" section.

Making the Connection

Oracle, like all client-server DBMSs, requires that you login to the DBMS before being able to issue commands. Login names might not be the same as your network login name (assuming that you are using a network); Oracle maintains its own list of users internally, and associates rights with each. For a database client, like Oracle SQL Developer, to connect to the Oracle server (even a local Oracle server), you must tell it where to find the server, and how to log in.

To connect Oracle SQL Developer to the Oracle server, follow these steps:

1. Run Oracle SQL Developer.

2. When the application loads, you see a screen split into three sections, with menus and an icon toolbar on top. The top-left

window is the Connections window, and it lists any defined Oracle servers (of which there will currently be none).

3. At the top of the Connections window, click on the green + button to add a new database connection.
4. For Connection Name, enter `crashcourse`. (The name does not have to match the database, workspace, login, or anything else; this is just the name that Oracle SQL Developer uses to identify each defined connection.)
5. For Username and Password, enter what you specified when you created the database instance or workspace previously.
6. Check the Save Password checkbox so that you don't have to keep entering the password.
7. For Hostname, enter `localhost` if you are using your own local Oracle server. If you are using a remote or hosted server, enter the hostname given to you by that server's administrator.
8. SID is the database instance id. If you are using a local Oracle server and followed the preceding steps, then this is `crashcourse` if you have a dedicated Oracle instance, or `xe` if you are using your own workspace with the single Oracle Express Edition instance.
9. Click the Test button.
10. At the bottom left of the dialog box, you should see `Status : Success`. If that is displayed, click the Save button to save this new connection. If an error message is displayed, check the form fields and correct the error before proceeding.

After you save the new `crashcourse` connection, you should see it listed in the Connections window on the top right. You can now close the dialog box.

> NOTE: **Using Other Clients**
>
> If you are using a client other than Oracle SQL Developer, you still need to provide this information to connect to Oracle. The exact steps might differ, but the same information is required.

A Quick Introduction to Oracle SQL Developer

You'll be using Oracle SQL Developer extensively as you learn PL/SQL, so it's worth taking a moment to familiarize yourself with this tool:

> NOTE: **Just the Basics**
>
> Oracle SQL Developer is a powerful database client, and we'll just use basic query execution capabilities in this book. In the future, as you use more of Oracle's capabilities, it would be to your advantage to learn more about this tool.

- Click the + next to your new `crashcourse` connection to expand it. This shows you all tables, views, and much more. You can further expand into each menu option, and can right-click on each to edit and more.
- The most important part of the screen is the large area on the right. This is where you enter your PL/SQL statements and display results (if there are any).
- When you open a connection, a worksheet should automatically open for you to start entering SQL. If it does not, or if you want multiple worksheets open, you can click on the SQL Worksheet button in the application toolbar (it's the one with a green icon and the word *SQL* in black on white in front of it). Click OK and you'll have another worksheet to use.
- Let's give it a try. Enter the following PL/SQL in the Worksheet screen. (Don't worry if the code doesn't make sense; it will within the next few lessons.)

  ```
  SELECT TO_CHAR(SYSDATE, 'DD-MON-YYYY HH:MI:SS') FROM DUAL;
  ```

  Click the Run Script button (it's the one with a green arrow on top of a document; it should be the second from the left in the toolbar above the Worksheet window) to execute the SQL statement. You should see the system date and time displayed in a Query Result screen below.

- Lastly, when the screens get cluttered, click on the Clear button (the one with the picture of a pencil eraser) above either screen to clear the contents.

> **Execute** SQL developers often use the terms *execute* and *run* interchangeably; both mean actually running the SQL.

> NOTE: **Run Statement vs. Run Script**
>
> I just had you click the Run Script button to execute the SQL statements in the Worksheet window. Run Script does exactly that—it runs the entire script, every line of code in the worksheet. At times, however, you might want to run just part of a script, perhaps a single statement. To do this, you can use the Run Statement button instead (it has a green right-facing arrow); it runs whatever is currently selected in the Worksheet screen, rather than the entire script.

> TIP: **Using Multiple Worksheets**
>
> You now know how to open multiple Worksheet screens at once. You'll find doing so useful when you are working on and testing multiple SQL statements at the same time.

With that, you're ready to run some important SQL scripts—the ones used to create and populate the example tables that you'll be using in future lessons.

Creating and Populating the Example Tables

The tables used throughout this book are part of an order entry system used by an imaginary distributor of paraphernalia that might be needed by your favorite cartoon characters (yes, cartoon characters; no one said that learning Oracle had to be boring). The tables are used to perform several tasks, including:

- Manage vendors
- Manage product catalogs

- Manage customer lists
- Enter customer orders

Making this all work requires six tables that are closely interconnected as part of a relational database design. Here are the tables we'll be using:

- The `customers` table contains your customers.
- The `orders` table contains one row per order placed.
- The `orderitems` table contains the details for each item in an order (the orders in the `orders` table).
- The `products` table lists all available products from all vendors.
- The `productnotes` table contains notes pertaining to products.
- The `vendors` table contains product vendors.

These six tables contain multiple columns, and are all connected using foreign keys. A detailed description of each of the tables appears in Appendix A, "The Example Tables."

> NOTE: **Simplified Examples**
>
> The tables used here are by no means complete. A real-world order entry system would have to keep track of lots of other data that has not been included here (for example, payment and accounting information, shipment tracking, and more). However, these tables do demonstrate the kinds of data organization and relationships you encounter in most real installations. You can apply these techniques and technologies to your own databases.

Obtaining the Same Table Scripts

To follow along with the examples, you need a set of populated tables. Everything you need to get up and running can be found on this book's web page at `http://forta.com/books/0672328666`.

The web page contains a ZIP file that you should download. Inside it are two SQL script files:

- `create.sql` contains the PL/SQL statements to create the six database tables (including defining all primary keys and foreign key constraints).
- `populate.sql` contains the PL/SQL `INSERT` statements used to populate these tables with sample data.

> NOTE: **For Oracle Only**
>
> The SQL statements in the downloadable `.sql` files are very DBMS specific, and are designed to be used only with Oracle.

After you have downloaded the scripts, you can use them to create and populate the tables needed to follow along with the lessons in this book.

> NOTE: **Create, Then Populate**
>
> You must run the table creation scripts *before* the table population scripts. Be sure to check for any error messages returned by these scripts. If the creation scripts fail, you need to remedy whatever problem might exist before continuing with table population.

Create the Tables

Database tables are created using the SQL statement `CREATE TABLE`, but rather than have you type that all out, you can use the `create.sql` file that you downloaded.

1. Make sure Oracle SQL Developer is open and the `crashcourse` connection is open.
2. Use the Open button (it has a picture of a yellow folder) or choose File, Open to open `create.sql`. The contents of `create.sql` appear in a new worksheet.
3. Because you could be working with multiple database connections, you need to tell Oracle SQL Developer to use the `crashcourse` connection. From the drop-down box at the top right above the Worksheet screen, select `crashcourse`.

4. Click the Run Script button (once again, it's the one above the Worksheet screen; a green arrow over a document). You should then see the following output:

Output ▼

```
table CUSTOMERS created.
table ORDERITEMS created.
table ORDERS created.
table PRODUCTS created.
table VENDORS created.
table PRODUCTNOTES created.
table CUSTOMERS altered.
table ORDERITEMS altered.
table ORDERS altered.
table PRODUCTS altered.
table VENDORS altered.
table PRODUCTNOTES altered.
table ORDERITEMS altered.
table ORDERITEMS altered.
table ORDERS altered.
table PRODUCTS altered.
table PRODUCTNOTES altered.
```

The preceding tells you that six tables were created, and that they were then also altered (we do this to add primary and foreign keys). Now that you have tables, let's populate them.

Populate the Tables

Data is inserted into a table using the `INSERT` statement. Once again, rather than typing hundreds of lines of SQL, we'll use the downloaded file instead.

1. Use the Open button (or choose File, Open) to open `populate.sql`. The contents of `populate.sql` appear in a new worksheet.

2. Make sure that `crashcourse` is selected in the drop-down box at the top right above the Worksheet screen.

3. Click the Run Script button (once again, it's the one above the Worksheet screen; a green arrow over a document). You should then see the following message appear 55 times (once for each row inserted):

Output ▼

```
1 rows inserted.
```

You now have the tables and data you need to proceed.

One More Look at Oracle SQL Developer

Before finishing this lesson, I want to point out one more invaluable feature of Oracle SQL Developer. Now that you have created and populated the example tables, try the following:

1. Locate the `crashcourse` database connection in the Connections screen, and click + to expand it.
2. The first item displayed is b; click + to expand that.
3. Scroll through the list of tables to find one that we just created. The first one you'll see is `customers`, but any of our tables will do.
4. Click the + to expand the table, and see the table column names.

In addition, Oracle SQL Developer opens a new tab in the main Worksheet area and the table columns (showing details about type, nullable, and more). Above the data are other tabs that you can click on—Data shows the contents of the table, Constraints lists primary and foreign keys and any other defined constraints, Details lists all sorts of information about the table and how it is being used, SQL lists SQL code that could be used to create the table, and so on. Feel free to browse around; this data and view are useful for working with Oracle.

Summary

In this lesson, you learned how to connect and log in to Oracle, and how to enter and execute SQL statements. You also created and populated the example tables. Armed with this knowledge, you can now dig in to the all-important `SELECT` statement.

LESSON 4

Retrieving Data

In this lesson, you'll learn how to use the SELECT *statement to retrieve one or more columns of data from a table.*

The SELECT Statement

> NOTE: **Sample Tables Required**
>
> From this point on, all lessons use the sample database tables. If you have yet to install these, please refer to Lesson 3, "Working with Oracle," before proceeding.

As explained in Lesson 1, "Understanding SQL," SQL statements are made up of plain English terms. These terms are called *keywords*, and every SQL statement is made up of one or more keywords. The SQL statement you'll probably use most frequently is the SELECT statement. Its purpose is to retrieve information from one or more tables.

To use SELECT to retrieve table data, you must, at a minimum, specify two pieces of information—what you want to select, and from where you want to select it.

Retrieving Individual Columns

We'll start with a simple SQL SELECT statement, as follows:

Input ▼

```
SELECT prod_name
FROM products;
```

> TIP: **Type Then Execute**
>
> By now it should be obvious, but I'll remind you one last time. Type the SQL code in the Oracle SQL Developer Worksheet screen, and then click the Run Script button to execute it. Results appear in a screen below the Worksheet. If you need more room, you can drag and resize all the screens.

Analysis ▼

The previous statement uses the `SELECT` statement to retrieve a single column called `prod_name` from the `products` table. The desired column name is specified right after the `SELECT` keyword, and the `FROM` keyword specifies the name of the table from which to retrieve the data. The following shows the output from this statement:

Output ▼

```
+-----------------+
| prod_name       |
+-----------------+
| .5 ton anvil    |
| 1 ton anvil     |
| 2 ton anvil     |
| Oil can         |
| Fuses           |
| Sling           |
| TNT (1 stick)   |
| TNT (5 sticks)  |
| Bird seed       |
| Carrots         |
| Safe            |
| Detonator       |
| JetPack 1000    |
| JetPack 2000    |
+-----------------+
```

> NOTE: **Unsorted Data**
>
> If you tried this query yourself, you might have discovered that the data displayed in a different order than shown here. If this is the case, don't worry—it is working exactly as it is supposed to. If

> query results are not explicitly sorted (we'll get to that in the next lesson), data will be returned in no order of any significance. It might be the order in which the data was added to the table, but it might not. As long as your query returned the same number of rows, then it is working.

A simple `SELECT` statement like the one just shown returns all the rows in a table. Data is not filtered (so as to retrieve a subset of the results), nor is it sorted. We'll discuss these topics in the next few lessons.

> NOTE: **Terminating Statements**
>
> Multiple SQL statements must be separated by semicolons (the `;` character). Oracle (like most DBMSs) does not require that a semicolon be specified after single statements. That said, most SQL developers get in the habit of always terminating their SQL statements with semicolons, even when they are not needed.

> NOTE: **SQL Statements and Case**
>
> Note that SQL statements are not case sensitive, so `SELECT` is the same as `select`, which is the same as `Select`. Many SQL developers find that using uppercase for all SQL keywords and lowercase for column and table names makes code easier to read and debug.
>
> However, be aware that while the SQL language is not case sensitive, identifiers (the names of databases, tables, and columns) might be. As a best practice, pick a case convention, and use it consistently.

> TIP: **Use of White Space**
>
> All extra white space within a SQL statement is ignored when that statement is processed. You can specify SQL statements on one long line or break them up over many lines. Most SQL developers find that breaking up statements over multiple lines makes them easier to read and debug.

Retrieving Multiple Columns

To retrieve multiple columns from a table, you use the same SELECT statement. The only difference is that you must specify multiple column names after the SELECT keyword, and separate each column by a comma.

> TIP: **Take Care with Commas**
>
> When selecting multiple columns, be sure to specify a comma between each column name, but not after the last column name. Doing so generates an error.

The following SELECT statement retrieves three columns from the products table:

Input ▼

```
SELECT prod_id, prod_name, prod_price
FROM products;
```

Analysis ▼

Just as in the prior example, this statement uses the SELECT statement to retrieve data from the products table. In this example, three column names are specified, each separated by a comma. The output from this statement is as follows:

Output ▼

```
+---------+-----------------+------------+
| prod_id | prod_name       | prod_price |
+---------+-----------------+------------+
| ANV01   | .5 ton anvil    |       5.99 |
| ANV02   | 1 ton anvil     |       9.99 |
| ANV03   | 2 ton anvil     |      14.99 |
| OL1     | Oil can         |       8.99 |
| FU1     | Fuses           |       3.42 |
| SLING   | Sling           |       4.49 |
| TNT1    | TNT (1 stick)   |        2.5 |
| TNT2    | TNT (5 sticks)  |         10 |
| FB      | Bird seed       |         10 |
```

```
| FC       | Carrots          |         2.5 |
| SAFE     | Safe             |          50 |
| DTNTR    | Detonator        |          13 |
| JP1000   | JetPack 1000     |          35 |
| JP2000   | JetPack 2000     |          55 |
+----------+------------------+-------------+
```

> NOTE: **Presentation of Data**
>
> SQL statements typically return raw, unformatted data. Data formatting is a presentation issue, not a retrieval issue. Therefore, presentation (for example, alignment and displaying the price values as currency amounts with the currency symbol and commas) is typically specified in the application that displays the data. Actual raw retrieved data (without application-provided formatting) is rarely displayed as is.

Retrieving All Columns

In addition to being able to specify desired columns (one or more, as shown previously), you can also use SELECT statements to request all columns without having to list them individually. This is done using the asterisk (*) wildcard character in lieu of actual column names, as follows:

Input ▼

```
SELECT *
FROM products;
```

Analysis ▼

When you specify a wildcard (*), all the columns in the table are returned. The columns are in the order in which the columns appear in the table definition. However, you cannot rely on this because changes to table schemas (adding and removing columns, for example) could cause ordering changes.

> CAUTION: **Using Wildcards**
>
> As a rule, you are better off not using the * wildcard unless you really do need every column in the table. Even though use of wildcards might save you the time and effort needed to list the desired columns explicitly, retrieving unnecessary columns usually slows down the performance of your retrieval and your application.

> TIP: **Retrieving Unknown Columns**
>
> There is one big advantage to using wildcards. As you do not explicitly specify column names (because the asterisk retrieves every column), it is possible to retrieve columns whose names are unknown.

Retrieving Distinct Rows

As you have seen, `SELECT` returns all matched rows. But what if you did not want every occurrence of every value? For example, suppose you wanted the vendor ID of all vendors with products in your `products` table:

Input ▼

```
SELECT vend_id
FROM products;
```

Output ▼

```
+---------+
| vend_id |
+---------+
|    1001 |
|    1001 |
|    1001 |
|    1002 |
|    1002 |
|    1003 |
|    1003 |
|    1003 |
|    1003 |
```

```
|    1003 |
|    1003 |
|    1003 |
|    1005 |
|    1005 |
+---------+
```

The `SELECT` statement returned 14 rows (even though only 4 vendors are in that list) because 14 products are listed in the `products` table. So how could you retrieve a list of distinct values?

The solution is to use the `DISTINCT` keyword which, as its name implies, instructs Oracle to only return distinct values:

Input ▼

```
SELECT DISTINCT vend_id
FROM products;
```

Analysis ▼

`SELECT DISTINCT vend_id` tells Oracle to only return distinct (unique) `vend_id` rows, and so only 4 rows are returned, as shown in the following output. If you use it, you must place the `DISTINCT` keyword directly in front of the column names:

Output ▼

```
+---------+
| vend_id |
+---------+
|    1001 |
|    1002 |
|    1003 |
|    1005 |
+---------+
```

> CAUTION: **Can't Be Partially** `DISTINCT`
>
> The `DISTINCT` keyword applies to all columns, not just the one it precedes. If you were to specify `SELECT DISTINCT vend_id, prod_price`, all rows would be retrieved unless *both* of the specified columns were distinct.

Using Fully Qualified Table Names

The SQL examples used thus far have referred to columns by just the column names. Referring to columns using fully qualified names (using both the table and column names) is also possible. Look at this example:

Input ▼

```
SELECT products.prod_name
FROM products;
```

This SQL statement is functionally identical to the first one used in this lesson, but here a fully qualified column name is specified.

Table names, too, may be fully qualified, as shown here:

Input ▼

```
SELECT products.prod_name
FROM crashcourse.products;
```

Once again, this statement is functionally identical to the one just used (assuming, of course, that the `products` table is indeed in the `crashcourse` database).

Situations exist where fully qualified names are required, as we will see in later lessons. For now, it is worth noting this syntax so you'll know what it is if you run across it.

Using Comments

As you have seen, SQL statements are instructions that Oracle processes. But what if you wanted to include text that you do not want processed and executed? Why would you ever want to do this? Here are a few reasons:

- The SQL statements we've been using here are all very short and very simple. But, as your SQL statement grows (in length and complexity), you'll want to include descriptive comments (for your own future reference or for whoever has to work on the project next). You need to embed these comments in the SQL scripts, but they are obviously not intended for Oracle processing. (For an example of this, see the `create.sql` and `populate.sql` files you used in Lesson 3.)

- The same is true for headers at the top of a SQL file, perhaps containing the programmer contact information and a description and notes. (You also see this use case in the `create.sql` and `populate.sql` files.)
- Another important use for comments is to temporarily stop SQL code from being executed. If you were working with a long SQL statement and wanted to test just part of it, you could *comment out* some of the code so that Oracle saw it as comments and ignored it.

Oracle supports two forms of comment syntax. We'll start with inline comments:

Input ▼

```
SELECT prod_name    -- this is a comment
FROM products;
```

Analysis ▼

You may embed comments inline using `--` (two hyphens). Anything after the `--` is considered comment text, making this a good option for describing columns in a `CREATE TABLE` statement, for example.

Here is another form of inline comment:

Input ▼

```
-- This is a comment
SELECT prod_name
FROM products;
```

Analysis ▼

A `--` at the start of a line makes the entire line a comment. You can see this format comment used in the accompanying `create.sql` and `populate.sql` scripts.

You can also create multi-line comments, and comments that stop and start anywhere within the script:

Input ▼

```
/* SELECT prod_name, vend_id
FROM products; */

SELECT prod_name
FROM products;
```

Analysis ▼

`/*` starts a comment, and `*/` ends it. Anything between `/*` and `*/` is comment text. This type of comment is often used to *comment out* code, as shown in this example. Here, two `SELECT` statements are defined, but the first won't execute because it has been commented out.

> TIP: **Oracle SQL Developer Color Coding**
>
> You might have noticed that Oracle SQL Developer color codes your PL/SQL. SQL statements are usually displayed in blue, identifiers (like table and column names) are in black, and so on. Color coding makes it easier to read your code and to find mistakes; if you've mistyped a PL/SQL statement, it'll probably appear in the wrong color. Oracle SQL Developer also color codes any comments (inline or multi-line) and displays them in a light gray. This makes it easy to locate comments and commented-out code (and can also help you find code that you no longer want commented out).

Summary

In this lesson, you learned how to use the SQL `SELECT` statement to retrieve a single table column, multiple table columns, and all table columns. You also learned about commenting and saw various ways that you can use comments. In the next lesson, you'll learn how to sort the retrieved data.

LESSON 5
Sorting Retrieved Data

This lesson shows you how to use the `SELECT` *statement's* `ORDER BY` *clause to sort retrieved data as needed.*

Sorting Data

As you learned in the last lesson, the following SQL statement returns a single column from a database table. But look at the output. The data appears to be displayed in no particular order at all:

Input ▼

```
SELECT prod_name
FROM products;
```

Output ▼

```
+-----------------+
| prod_name       |
+-----------------+
| .5 ton anvil    |
| 1 ton anvil     |
| 2 ton anvil     |
| Oil can         |
| Fuses           |
| Sling           |
| TNT (1 stick)   |
| TNT (5 sticks)  |
| Bird seed       |
| Carrots         |
| Safe            |
| Detonator       |
| JetPack 1000    |
| JetPack 2000    |
+-----------------+
```

Actually, the retrieved data is not in a mere random order. If unsorted, data typically displays in the order in which it appears in the underlying tables. This could be the order in which the data was added to the tables initially. However, if data was subsequently updated or deleted, the order is affected by how Oracle reuses reclaimed storage space. The end result is that you cannot (and should not) rely on the sort order if you do not explicitly control it. Relational database design theory states that the sequence of retrieved data cannot be assumed to have significance if ordering was not explicitly specified.

> **Clause** SQL statements are made up of clauses, some required and some optional. A clause usually consists of a keyword and supplied data. An example of this is the `SELECT` statement's `FROM` clause, which you saw in the last lesson.

To explicitly sort data retrieved using a `SELECT` statement, you use the `ORDER BY` clause. `ORDER BY` takes the name of one or more columns by which to sort the output. Look at the following example:

Input ▼

```
SELECT prod_name
FROM products
ORDER BY prod_name;
```

Analysis ▼

This statement is identical to the earlier statement, except it also specifies an `ORDER BY` clause instructing Oracle to sort the data alphabetically by the `prod_name` column. The results are the following:

Output ▼

```
+----------------+
| prod_name      |
+----------------+
| .5 ton anvil   |
| 1 ton anvil    |
| 2 ton anvil    |
| Bird seed      |
| Carrots        |
```

```
| Detonator      |
| Fuses          |
| JetPack 1000   |
| JetPack 2000   |
| Oil can        |
| Safe           |
| Sling          |
| TNT (1 stick)  |
| TNT (5 sticks) |
+----------------+
```

> TIP: **Sorting by Nonselected Columns**
>
> More often than not, the columns used in an `ORDER BY` clause are ones that were selected for display. However, this is actually not required, and sorting data by a column that is not retrieved is perfectly legal.

Sorting by Multiple Columns

Sorting data by more than one column is often necessary. For example, you might want to display an employee list sorted by last name and first name (first sort by last name, and then within each last name sort by first name). This is useful if multiple employees have the same last name.

To sort by multiple columns, simply specify the column names separated by commas (just as you do when you are selecting multiple columns).

The following code retrieves three columns and sorts the results by two of them—first by price and then by name:

Input ▼

```
SELECT prod_id, prod_price, prod_name
FROM products
ORDER BY prod_price, prod_name;
```

Output ▼

```
+---------+------------+----------------+
| prod_id | prod_price | prod_name      |
+---------+------------+----------------+
| FC      |        2.5 | Carrots        |
```

```
| TNT1     |       2.5 | TNT (1 stick)  |
| FU1      |      3.42 | Fuses          |
| SLING    |      4.49 | Sling          |
| ANV01    |      5.99 | .5 ton anvil   |
| OL1      |      8.99 | Oil can        |
| ANV02    |      9.99 | 1 ton anvil    |
| FB       |        10 | Bird seed      |
| TNT2     |        10 | TNT (5 sticks) |
| DTNTR    |        13 | Detonator      |
| ANV03    |     14.99 | 2 ton anvil    |
| JP1000   |        35 | JetPack 1000   |
| SAFE     |        50 | Safe           |
| JP2000   |        55 | JetPack 2000   |
+----------+-----------+----------------+
```

You should understand that when you sort by multiple columns, the sort sequence is exactly as specified. In other words, using the output in the previous example, the products are sorted by the `prod_name` column only when multiple rows have the same `prod_price` value. If all the values in the `prod_price` column had been unique, no data would have been sorted by `prod_name`.

As you've seen, `ORDER BY` sorts results by columns, the names of which are provided in a comma-delimited list. Oracle also allows you to specify the sort order by referring to the column position in the `SELECT` statement. Here is the SQL statement we just used:

Input ▼

```
SELECT prod_id, prod_price, prod_name
FROM products
ORDER BY prod_price, prod_name;
```

What follows is the same SQL statement, but with a slightly different look at the `ORDER BY` clause:

Input ▼

```
SELECT prod_id, prod_price, prod_name
FROM products
ORDER BY 2, 3;
```

Analysis ▼

Instead of specifying column names, `ORDER BY 2, 3` instructs Oracle to sort by the second and third columns in the `SELECT` statement, namely `prod_price` and `prod_name`. Either way, the output is the same.

> TIP: **Use Sequence Number Ordering with Care**
>
> The type of `ORDER BY` just shown, where `SELECT` column position is used instead of column names, is referred to as *ordering by sequence number*. I show you this syntax so that you'll know what it is if you run across it. But, in general, using this type of `ORDER BY` statement is risky, because if you ever change the `SELECT` statement, you might inadvertently break your ordering. As a rule, being explicit is always better.

Specifying Sort Direction

Data sorting is not limited to ascending sort orders (from `A` to `Z`). Although this is the default sort order, you can also use the `ORDER BY` clause to sort in descending order (from `Z` to `A`). To sort by descending order, you must specify the keyword `DESC`.

The following example sorts the products by price in descending order (most expensive first):

Input ▼

```
SELECT prod_id, prod_price, prod_name
FROM products
ORDER BY prod_price DESC;
```

Output ▼

```
+---------+------------+---------------+
| prod_id | prod_price | prod_name     |
+---------+------------+---------------+
| JP2000  |         55 | JetPack 2000  |
| SAFE    |         50 | Safe          |
| JP1000  |         35 | JetPack 1000  |
| ANV03   |      14.99 | 2 ton anvil   |
```

```
| DTNTR    |          13 | Detonator      |
| TNT2     |          10 | TNT (5 sticks) |
| FB       |          10 | Bird seed      |
| ANV02    |        9.99 | 1 ton anvil    |
| OL1      |        8.99 | Oil can        |
| ANV01    |        5.99 | .5 ton anvil   |
| SLING    |        4.49 | Sling          |
| FU1      |        3.42 | Fuses          |
| FC       |         2.5 | Carrots        |
| TNT1     |         2.5 | TNT (1 stick)  |
+----------+------------+----------------+
```

But what if you were to sort by multiple columns? The following example sorts the products in descending order (most expensive first), plus product name:

Input ▼

```
SELECT prod_id, prod_price, prod_name
FROM products
ORDER BY prod_price DESC, prod_name;
```

Output ▼

```
+----------+------------+----------------+
| prod_id  | prod_price | prod_name      |
+----------+------------+----------------+
| JP2000   |          55 | JetPack 2000   |
| SAFE     |          50 | Safe           |
| JP1000   |          35 | JetPack 1000   |
| ANV03    |       14.99 | 2 ton anvil    |
| DTNTR    |          13 | Detonator      |
| FB       |          10 | Bird seed      |
| TNT2     |          10 | TNT (5 sticks) |
| ANV02    |        9.99 | 1 ton anvil    |
| OL1      |        8.99 | Oil can        |
| ANV01    |        5.99 | .5 ton anvil   |
| SLING    |        4.49 | Sling          |
| FU1      |        3.42 | Fuses          |
| FC       |         2.5 | Carrots        |
| TNT1     |         2.5 | TNT (1 stick)  |
+----------+------------+----------------+
```

Analysis ▼

The DESC keyword only applies to the column name that directly precedes it. In the previous example, DESC was specified for the prod_price column, but not for the prod_name column. Therefore, the prod_price column is sorted in descending order, but the prod_name column (within each price) is still sorted in standard ascending order.

> TIP: **Sorting Descending on Multiple Columns**
>
> If you want to sort descending on multiple columns, be sure each column has its own DESC keyword.

The opposite of DESC is ASC (for *ascending*), which you may specify to sort in ascending order. In practice, however, you don't usually use ASC because ascending order is the default sequence (and is assumed if neither ASC nor DESC are specified).

> TIP: **Case Sensitivity and Sort Orders**
>
> When you sort textual data, is A the same as a? And does a come before B or after Z? These are not theoretical questions, and the answers depend on how the database is set up.
>
> In *dictionary* sort order, A is treated the same as a, and that is the default behavior in Oracle (and indeed most DBMSs). However, administrators can change this behavior if needed. (If your database contains lots of foreign language characters, this might become necessary.)
>
> The key here is that, if you do need an alternate sort order, you cannot accomplish it with a simple ORDER BY clause. You must contact your database administrator.

Summary

In this lesson, you learned how to sort retrieved data using the SELECT statement's ORDER BY clause. You can use this clause, which must be the last in the SELECT statement, to sort data on one or more columns as needed.

LESSON 6

Filtering Data

This lesson shows you how to use the `SELECT` statement's `WHERE` clause to specify search conditions.

Using the `WHERE` Clause

Database tables usually contain large amounts of data, and you seldom need to retrieve all the rows in a table. More often than not, you'll want to extract a subset of the table's data as needed for specific operations or reports. Retrieving just the data you want involves specifying *search criteria*, also known as a *filter condition.*

Within a `SELECT` statement, you filter data by specifying search criteria in the `WHERE` clause. You specify the `WHERE` clause right after the table name (the `FROM` clause), as follows:

Input ▼

```
SELECT prod_name, prod_price
FROM products
WHERE prod_price = 2.50;
```

Analysis ▼

This statement retrieves two columns from the `products` table, but instead of returning all rows, only rows with a `prod_price` value of `2.50` are returned, as follows:

Output ▼

```
+---------------+-------------+
| prod_name     | prod_price  |
+---------------+-------------+
| Carrots       |         2.5 |
| TNT (1 stick) |         2.5 |
+---------------+-------------+
```

> NOTE: **No `ORDER BY` Clause Specified**
>
> In the interests of saving space (and your typing), I omitted the `ORDER BY` clause in many of these examples. As such, it is entirely possible that your output won't exactly match the output in the book. Although the number of returned rows should always match, their order might not. Of course, feel free to add an `ORDER BY` clause if you want; it needs to go after the `WHERE` clause.

> NOTE: **Decimal Rounding**
>
> Even though the `WHERE` clause specified a value of `2.50`, your returned data might show the value rounded to `2.5` (as it did for me). Oracle, like all DBMSs, has default behaviors for how it formats returned data, and the result might not always be exactly what you want. In Lesson 11, "Using Data Manipulation Functions," you learn how to use functions to format data exactly as needed.

This example uses a simple equality test: It checks to see whether a column has a specified value, and it filters the data accordingly. However, SQL enables you to do more than just test for equality.

> TIP: **SQL Versus Application Filtering**
>
> You can also filter data at the application level. To do this, the SQL `SELECT` statement retrieves more data than is actually required for the client application, and the client code loops through the returned data to extract just the needed rows.

As a rule, this practice is strongly discouraged. Databases are optimized to perform filtering quickly and efficiently. Making the client application (or development language) do the database's job dramatically impacts application performance and creates applications that cannot scale properly. In addition, if data is filtered at the client, the server has to send unneeded data across the network connections, resulting in a waste of network bandwidth resources.

CAUTION: WHERE **Clause Position**

When using both ORDER BY and WHERE clauses, make sure ORDER BY comes after the WHERE; otherwise, an error is generated. (See Lesson 5, "Sorting Retrieved Data," for more information on using ORDER BY.)

The WHERE Clause Operators

The first WHERE clause we looked at tests for equality—determining whether a column contains a specific value. Oracle supports a whole range of conditional operators, some of which Table 6.1 lists.

TABLE 6.1 WHERE Clause Operators

Operator	Description
=	Equality
<>	Nonequality
!=	Nonequality
<	Less than
<=	Less than or equal to
>	Greater than
>=	Greater than or equal to
BETWEEN	Between two specified values

Checking Against a Single Value

We have already seen an example of testing for equality. Here's one more:

Input ▼

```
SELECT prod_name, prod_price
FROM products
WHERE prod_name = 'Fuses';
```

Output ▼

```
+-----------+------------+
| prod_name | prod_price |
+-----------+------------+
| Fuses     |       3.42 |
+-----------+------------+
```

Analysis ▼

Checking for `WHERE prod_name = 'Fuses'` returned a single row with a value of `Fuses`.

Depending on how your Oracle server is configured, Oracle could be case sensitive when performing matches, in which case `fuses` and `Fuses` would not be the same. Try this example:

Input ▼

```
SELECT prod_name, prod_price
FROM products
WHERE prod_name = 'fuses';
```

Analysis ▼

By default, Oracle is case sensitive, and so comparing to lowercase `fuses` returns no results, because `fuses` and `Fuses` are not the same.

> TIP: **Case Insensitive Equality Comparisons**
>
> So how can you find `fuses`, `Fuses`, `FUSES`, and any other mix of upper- and lowercase? The trick is to use functions to change everything to one case, either upper or lower. You'll learn about string manipulation functions in Lesson 10, "Creating Calculated Fields."

Now look at a few examples to demonstrate the use of other operators.

This first example lists all products that cost less than `10`:

Input ▼

```
SELECT prod_name, prod_price
FROM products
WHERE prod_price < 10;
```

Output ▼

```
+--------------+------------+
| prod_name    | prod_price |
+--------------+------------+
| .5 ton anvil |       5.99 |
| 1 ton anvil  |       9.99 |
| Carrots      |        2.5 |
| Fuses        |       3.42 |
| Oil can      |       8.99 |
| Sling        |       4.49 |
| TNT (1 stick) |       2.5 |
+--------------+------------+
```

This next statement retrieves all products costing `10` or less (resulting in two additional matches):

Input ▼

```
SELECT prod_name, prod_price
FROM products
WHERE prod_price <= 10;
```

Output ▼

```
+----------------+------------+
| prod_name      | prod_price |
+----------------+------------+
| .5 ton anvil   |       5.99 |
| 1 ton anvil    |       9.99 |
| Bird seed      |         10 |
| Carrots        |        2.5 |
| Fuses          |       3.42 |
| Oil can        |       8.99 |
| Sling          |       4.49 |
| TNT (1 stick)  |        2.5 |
| TNT (5 sticks) |         10 |
+----------------+------------+
```

Checking for Nonmatches

This next example lists all products not made by vendor `1003`:

Input ▼

```
SELECT vend_id, prod_name
FROM products
WHERE vend_id <> 1003;
```

Output ▼

```
+---------+--------------+
| vend_id | prod_name    |
+---------+--------------+
|    1001 | .5 ton anvil |
|    1001 | 1 ton anvil  |
|    1001 | 2 ton anvil  |
|    1002 | Fuses        |
|    1005 | JetPack 1000 |
|    1005 | JetPack 2000 |
|    1002 | Oil can      |
+---------+--------------+
```

> TIP: **When to Use Quotes**
>
> If you look closely at the conditions used in the examples' `WHERE` clauses, you will notice that some values are enclosed in single quotes (such as `'Fuses'` used previously), and others are not. You use single quotes to delimit strings. Comparing a value against a column that is a string *datatype* requires the delimiting quotes. You don't use quotes to delimit values used with numeric columns.

The following is the same example, except this one uses the `!=` operator instead of `<>`:

Input ▼

```
SELECT vend_id, prod_name
FROM products
WHERE vend_id != 1003;
```

> NOTE: `!=` **Versus** `<>`
>
> Yes, both `<>` and `!=` look for nonmatches. `!=` *means not equal to*, and `<>` means *less than or greater than* (in other words, *not equal to*). Use whichever you prefer.

Checking for a Range of Values

To check for a range of values, you can use the `BETWEEN` operator. Its syntax is a little different from other `WHERE` clause operators because it requires two values: the beginning and end of the range. You can use the `BETWEEN` operator, for example, to check for all products that cost between `5` and `10` or for all dates that fall between specified start and end dates.

The following example demonstrates the use of the `BETWEEN` operator by retrieving all products with a price between `5` and `10`:

Input ▼

```
SELECT prod_name, prod_price
FROM products
WHERE prod_price BETWEEN 5 AND 10;
```

Output ▼

```
+-----------------+------------+
| prod_name       | prod_price |
+-----------------+------------+
| .5 ton anvil    |       5.99 |
| 1 ton anvil     |       9.99 |
| Bird seed       |         10 |
| Oil can         |       8.99 |
| TNT (5 sticks)  |         10 |
+-----------------+------------+
```

Analysis ▼

As shown in this example, when you use `BETWEEN`, you must specify two values—the low end and high end of the desired range. You must also separate the two values by the `AND` keyword. `BETWEEN` matches all the values in the range, including the specified range start and end values.

Checking for No Value

When creating a table, the table designer can specify whether individual columns may contain no value. When a column contains no value, it is said to contain a `NULL` value. Columns destined to contain optional data are often created this way.

> **NULL** *No value*, as opposed to a field containing `0`, or an empty string, or just spaces.

The `SELECT` statement has a special `WHERE` clause that you can use to check for columns with `NULL` values—the `IS NULL` clause. The syntax looks like this:

Input ▼

```
SELECT prod_name
FROM products
WHERE prod_price IS NULL;
```

This statement returns a list of all products that have no price (an empty `prod_price` field, not a price of `0`), and because there are none, no data is returned. The `customers` table, however, does contain columns with `NULL` values—the `cust_email` column contains `NULL` if a customer has no email address on file:

Input ▼

```
SELECT cust_id
FROM customers
WHERE cust_email IS NULL;
```

Output ▼

```
+---------+
| cust_id |
+---------+
|   10002 |
|   10005 |
+---------+
```

> CAUTION: `NULL` **and Nonmatches**
>
> You might expect that when you filter to select all rows that do not have a particular value, rows with a `NULL` will be returned. But they will not. Because of the special meaning of *unknown*, the database does not know whether or not they match, and so they are not returned when filtering for matches or when filtering for non-matches.
>
> When filtering data, make sure to verify that the rows with a `NULL` in the filtered column are really present in the returned data.

Summary

In this lesson, you learned how to filter returned data using the `SELECT` statement's `WHERE` clause. You learned how to test for equality, non-equality, greater than and less than, value ranges, and `NULL` values.

LESSON 7
Advanced Data Filtering

This lesson shows you how to combine WHERE clauses to create powerful and sophisticated search conditions, and how to use the NOT and IN operators.

Combining WHERE Clauses

All the WHERE clauses introduced in Lesson 6, "Filtering Data," filter data on a single criterion. For a greater degree of filter control, Oracle allows you to specify multiple WHERE clauses. You may use these clauses in two ways: as AND clauses or as OR clauses.

> **Operator** A special keyword used to join or change clauses in a WHERE clause. Also known as *logical operators*.

Using the AND Operator

To filter by more than one column, you use the AND operator to append conditions to your WHERE clause. The following code demonstrates this:

Input ▼

```
SELECT prod_id, prod_price, prod_name
FROM products
WHERE vend_id = 1003 AND prod_price <= 10;
```

Analysis ▼

The preceding SQL statement retrieves the product name and price for all products made by vendor 1003 as long as the price is 10 or less. The WHERE clause in this SELECT statement is made up of two conditions, and the keyword AND is used to join them. AND instructs the DBMS to return only rows that meet all the conditions specified. If a product is made by vendor `1003` but it costs more than `10`, it is not retrieved. Similarly, products that cost less than `10` that are made by a vendor other than the one specified are not retrieved. The output generated by this SQL statement is as follows:

Output ▼

```
+---------+------------+----------------+
| prod_id | prod_price | prod_name      |
+---------+------------+----------------+
| FB      |         10 | Bird seed      |
| FC      |        2.5 | Carrots        |
| SLING   |       4.49 | Sling          |
| TNT1    |        2.5 | TNT (1 stick)  |
| TNT2    |         10 | TNT (5 sticks) |
+---------+------------+----------------+
```

> **AND** A keyword used in a `WHERE` clause to specify that only rows matching all the specified conditions should be retrieved.

The previous example contained a single `AND` clause and was thus made up of two filter conditions. You could use additional filter conditions as well, each separated by an `AND` keyword.

> NOTE: **No `ORDER BY` Clause Specified**
>
> As before, I omitted the `ORDER BY` clause in many of these examples. Feel free to add an `ORDER BY` clause if you want.

Using the OR Operator

The `OR` operator is exactly the opposite of `AND`. The `OR` operator instructs Oracle to retrieve rows that match either condition.

Look at the following `SELECT` statement:

Input ▼

```
SELECT prod_name, prod_price
FROM products
WHERE vend_id = 1002 OR vend_id = 1003;
```

Analysis ▼

The preceding SQL statement retrieves the product name and price for any products made by either of the two specified vendors. The OR operator tells the DBMS to match either condition, not both. If an AND operator had been used here, no data would be returned (it would have created a WHERE clause that could never be matched). The output generated by this SQL statement is as follows:

Output ▼

```
+----------------+------------+
| prod_name      | prod_price |
+----------------+------------+
| Detonator      |         13 |
| Bird seed      |         10 |
| Carrots        |        2.5 |
| Fuses          |       3.42 |
| Oil can        |       8.99 |
| Safe           |         50 |
| Sling          |       4.49 |
| TNT (1 stick)  |        2.5 |
| TNT (5 sticks) |         10 |
+----------------+------------+
```

> OR A keyword used in a WHERE clause to specify that any rows matching either of the specified conditions should be retrieved.

Understanding Order of Evaluation

WHERE clauses can contain any number of AND and OR operators. Combining the two enables you to perform sophisticated and complex filtering.

But combining AND and OR operators presents an interesting problem. To demonstrate this, look at an example. You need a list of all products costing 10 or more made by vendors 1002 and 1003. The following SELECT statement uses a combination of AND and OR operators to build a WHERE clause:

Input ▼

```
SELECT prod_name, prod_price
FROM products
WHERE vend_id = 1002 OR vend_id = 1003 AND prod_price >= 10;
```

Output ▼

```
+----------------+------------+
| prod_name      | prod_price |
+----------------+------------+
| Detonator      |         13 |
| Bird seed      |         10 |
| Fuses          |       3.42 |
| Oil can        |       8.99 |
| Safe           |         50 |
| TNT (5 sticks) |         10 |
+----------------+------------+
```

Analysis ▼

Look at the previously listed results. Two of the rows returned have prices less than `10`—so, obviously, the rows were not filtered as intended. Why did this happen? The answer is the order of evaluation. SQL (like most languages) processes `AND` operators before `OR` operators. When SQL sees the preceding `WHERE` clause, it reads *products made by vendor* `1002` *regardless of price, and any products costing* `10` *or more made by vendor* `1003`. In other words, because `AND` ranks higher in the order of evaluation, the wrong operators were joined together.

The solution to this problem is to use parentheses to explicitly group related operators. Take a look at the following `SELECT` statement and output:

Input ▼

```
SELECT prod_name, prod_price
FROM products
WHERE (vend_id = 1002 OR vend_id = 1003) AND prod_price >= 10;
```

Output ▼

```
+----------------+------------+
| prod_name      | prod_price |
+----------------+------------+
| Detonator      |         13 |
| Bird seed      |         10 |
| Safe           |         50 |
| TNT (5 sticks) |         10 |
+----------------+------------+
```

Analysis ▼

The only difference between this `SELECT` statement and the earlier one is that, in this statement, the first two `WHERE` clause conditions are enclosed within parentheses. Because parentheses have a higher order of evaluation than either `AND` or `OR` operators, the DBMS first filters the `OR` condition within those parentheses. The SQL statement then becomes *any products made by either vendor* `1002` *or vendor* `1003` *costing* `10` *or greater*, which is exactly what you want.

> TIP: **Using Parentheses in `WHERE` Clauses**
>
> Whenever you write `WHERE` clauses that use both `AND` and `OR` operators, use parentheses to explicitly group operators. Don't ever rely on the default evaluation order, even if it is exactly what you want. There is no downside to using parentheses, and you are always better off eliminating any ambiguity.

Using the `IN` Operator

Parentheses have another very different use in `WHERE` clauses. You use the `IN` operator to specify a range of conditions, any of which can be matched. `IN` takes a comma-delimited list of valid values, all enclosed within parentheses. The following example demonstrates this:

Input ▼

```
SELECT prod_name, prod_price
FROM products
WHERE vend_id IN (1002,1003)
ORDER BY prod_name;
```

Output ▼

```
+----------------+------------+
| prod_name      | prod_price |
+----------------+------------+
| Bird seed      |         10 |
| Carrots        |        2.5 |
| Detonator      |         13 |
| Fuses          |       3.42 |
| Oil can        |       8.99 |
| Safe           |         50 |
| Sling          |       4.49 |
| TNT (1 stick)  |        2.5 |
| TNT (5 sticks) |         10 |
+----------------+------------+
```

Analysis ▼

The `SELECT` statement retrieves all products made by vendor `1002` and vendor `1003`. A comma-delimited list of valid values follows the `IN` operator, and you must enclose the entire list within parentheses.

If you are thinking that the `IN` operator accomplishes the same goal as `OR`, you are right. The following SQL statement accomplishes the exact same thing as the previous example:

Input ▼

```
SELECT prod_name, prod_price
FROM products
WHERE vend_id = 1002 OR vend_id = 1003
ORDER BY prod_name;
```

Output ▼

```
+-----------------+------------+
| prod_name       | prod_price |
+-----------------+------------+
| Bird seed       |         10 |
| Carrots         |        2.5 |
| Detonator       |         13 |
| Fuses           |       3.42 |
| Oil can         |       8.99 |
| Safe            |         50 |
| Sling           |       4.49 |
| TNT (1 stick)   |        2.5 |
| TNT (5 sticks)  |         10 |
+-----------------+------------+
```

Why use the IN operator? The advantages are

- When you are working with long lists of valid options, the IN operator syntax is far cleaner and easier to read.
- The order of evaluation is easier to manage when you use IN (as there are fewer operators used).
- IN operators almost always execute more quickly than lists of OR operators (although you won't see any performance difference with very short lists like the ones used here).
- The biggest advantage of IN is that the IN operator can contain another SELECT statement, enabling you to build highly dynamic WHERE clauses. You'll look at this in detail in Lesson 14, "Working with Subqueries."

> **IN** A keyword used in a WHERE clause to specify a list of values to be matched using an OR comparison.

Using the NOT Operator

The WHERE clause's NOT operator has one function and one function only—NOT negates whatever condition comes next.

> **NOT** A keyword used in a WHERE clause to negate a condition.

The following example demonstrates the use of NOT. To list the products made by all vendors except vendors 1002 and 1003, you can use the following:

Input ▼

```
SELECT prod_name, prod_price
FROM products
WHERE vend_id NOT IN (1002,1003)
ORDER BY prod_name;
```

Output ▼

```
+--------------+------------+
| prod_name    | prod_price |
+--------------+------------+
| .5 ton anvil |       5.99 |
| 1 ton anvil  |       9.99 |
| 2 ton anvil  |      14.99 |
| JetPack 1000 |         35 |
| JetPack 2000 |         55 |
+--------------+------------+
```

Analysis ▼

The NOT here negates the condition that follows it; so instead of matching vend_id to 1002 or 1003, Oracle matches vend_id to anything that is not 1002 or 1003.

So why use NOT? Well, for simple WHERE clauses, really no advantage exists to using NOT. NOT is useful in more complex clauses. For example, using NOT in conjunction with an IN operator makes it simple to find all rows that do not match a list of criteria.

Summary

This lesson picked up where the last lesson left off and taught you how to combine WHERE clauses with the AND and OR operators. You also learned how to explicitly manage the order of evaluation, and how to use the IN and NOT operators.

LESSON 8
Using Wildcard Filtering

In this lesson, you'll learn what wildcards are, how to use them, and how to perform wildcard searches using the `LIKE` *operator for sophisticated filtering of retrieved data.*

Using the `LIKE` Operator

All the previous operators we studied filter against known values. Be it matching one or more values, testing for greater-than or less-than known values, or checking a range of values, the common denominator is that the values used in the filtering are known. But filtering data that way does not always work. For example, how could you search for all products that contained the text *anvil* within the product name? That cannot be done with simple comparison operators; that's a job for wildcard searching. Using wildcards, you can create search patterns that can be compared against your data. In this example, if you want to find all products that contain the words *anvil*, you could construct a wildcard search pattern enabling you to find that *anvil* text anywhere within a product name.

> **Wildcards** Special characters used to match parts of a value.

> **Search pattern** A search condition made up of literal text, wildcard characters, or any combination of the two.

The wildcards themselves are actually characters that have special meanings within SQL `WHERE` clauses, and SQL supports several wildcard types.

To use wildcards in search clauses, you must use the `LIKE` operator. `LIKE` instructs Oracle to compare the following search pattern using a wildcard match rather than a straight equality match.

> NOTE: **Predicates**
>
> When is an operator not an operator? When it is a *predicate*. Technically, `LIKE` is a predicate, not an operator. The end result is the same; just be aware of this term in case you run across it in the Oracle PL/SQL documentation.

Searching with the Percent Sign (%) Wildcard

The most frequently used wildcard is the percent sign (`%`). In a search string, `%` means *match any number of occurrences of any character*. For example, to find all products that start with the word `jet`, you can issue the following `SELECT` statement:

Input ▼

```
SELECT prod_id, prod_name
FROM products
WHERE prod_name LIKE 'Jet%';
```

Output ▼

```
+---------+---------------+
| prod_id | prod_name     |
+---------+---------------+
| JP1000  | JetPack 1000 |
| JP2000  | JetPack 2000 |
+---------+---------------+
```

Analysis ▼

This example uses a search pattern of `'Jet%'`. When this clause is evaluated, any value that starts with `Jet` is retrieved. The `%` tells Oracle to accept any characters after the word `Jet`, regardless of how many characters there are.

> NOTE: **Case-Sensitivity**
>
> As noted in Lesson 6, "Filtering Data," depending on how Oracle is configured, searches might be case sensitive, in which case `'jet%'` would not match `JetPack 1000`.

You can use wildcards anywhere in the search pattern, and use multiple wildcards as well. The following example uses two wildcards, one at either end of the pattern:

Input ▼

```
SELECT prod_id, prod_name
FROM products
WHERE prod_name LIKE '%anvil%';
```

Output ▼

```
+---------+--------------+
| prod_id | prod_name    |
+---------+--------------+
| ANV01   | .5 ton anvil |
| ANV02   | 1 ton anvil  |
| ANV03   | 2 ton anvil  |
+---------+--------------+
```

Analysis ▼

The search pattern `'%anvil%'` means *match any value that contains the text* `anvil` *anywhere within it, regardless of any characters before or after that text.*

You can also use wildcards in the middle of a search pattern, although that rarely tends to be useful.

It is important to note that, in addition to matching one or more characters, `%` also matches zero characters. `%` represents zero, one, or more characters at the specified location in the search pattern.

> NOTE: **Watch for Trailing Spaces**
>
> Trailing spaces can interfere with wildcard matching. For example, the clause `WHERE prod_name LIKE '%anvil'` might not match rows if there were additional characters after the final `l`. One simple solution to this problem is to always append a final `%` to the search pattern. A better solution is to trim the spaces using functions, discussed in Lesson 11, "Using Data Manipulation Functions."

> CAUTION: **Watch for** `NULL`
>
> Although it might seem that the `%` wildcard matches anything, there is one exception: `NULL`. Not even the clause `WHERE prod_name LIKE '%'` will match a row with the value `NULL` as the product name.

> TIP: **Searching for** `@`
>
> Here's a fun question. How would you create a search pattern to look for the text `@` itself (instead of `@` matching multiple characters)? The answer is to use two `@`'s, as in `@@`. This is known as *escaping*.

Searching with the Underscore (_) Wildcard

Another useful wildcard is the underscore (_). The underscore is used just like `%`, but instead of matching multiple characters, the underscore matches just a single character.

Take a look at this example:

Input ▼

```
SELECT prod_id, prod_name
FROM products
WHERE prod_name LIKE '_ ton anvil%';
```

Output ▼

```
+---------+-------------+
| prod_id | prod_name   |
+---------+-------------+
| ANV02   | 1 ton anvil |
| ANV03   | 2 ton anvil |
+---------+-------------+
```

Analysis ▼

The search pattern used in this `WHERE` clause specifies a wildcard followed by literal text. The results shown are the only rows that match the search pattern: The underscore matches `1` in the first row and `2` in the second row. The `.5 ton anvil` product did not match because the search pattern matched a single character, not two. The search pattern also ends with a wildcard, just to be safe (see the earlier "Watch for Trailing Spaces" note).

By contrast, the following `SELECT` statement uses the `%` wildcard and returns three matching products:

Input ▼

```
SELECT prod_id, prod_name
FROM products
WHERE prod_name LIKE '% ton anvil%';
```

Output ▼

```
+---------+--------------+
| prod_id | prod_name    |
+---------+--------------+
| ANV01   | .5 ton anvil |
| ANV02   | 1 ton anvil  |
| ANV03   | 2 ton anvil  |
+---------+--------------+
```

Unlike `%`, which can match zero characters, `_` always matches one character—no more and no less.

Tips for Using Wildcards

As you can see, Oracle's wildcards are extremely powerful. But that power comes with a price: Wildcard searches typically take far longer to process than any other search types discussed previously. Here are some tips to keep in mind when using wildcards:

- Don't overuse wildcards. If another search operator will do, use it instead.
- When you do use wildcards, try to not use them at the beginning of the search pattern unless absolutely necessary. Search patterns that begin with wildcards are the slowest to process.
- Pay careful attention to the placement of the wildcard symbols. If they are misplaced, you might not return the data you intended.

Having said that, wildcards are an important and useful search tool that you will use frequently.

Summary

In this lesson, you learned what wildcards are and how to use SQL wildcards in your `WHERE` clauses. You also learned that you should use wildcards carefully and never overuse them.

LESSON 9

Searching Using Regular Expressions

In this lesson, you'll learn how to use regular expressions within Oracle PL/SQL `WHERE` *clauses for greater control over data filtering.*

Understanding Regular Expressions

The filtering examples in the previous two lessons enabled you to locate data using matches, comparisons, and wildcard operators. For basic filtering (and even some not-so-basic filtering), this might be enough. But as the complexity of filtering conditions grows, so does the complexity of the `WHERE` clauses themselves.

And this is where regular expressions become useful. Regular expressions are part of a special language used to match text. If you needed to extract phone numbers from a text file, you might use a regular expression. If you needed to locate all files with digits in the middle of their names, you might use a regular expression. If you wanted to find all repeated words in a block of text, you might use a regular expression. And if you wanted to replace all URLs in a page with actual HTML links to those same URLs, yes, you might use a regular expression (or two, for this last example).

Regular expressions are supported in all sorts of programming languages, text editors, operating systems, and more. Savvy programmers and network managers have long regarded regular expressions as a vital component of their technical toolboxes.

Regular expressions are created using the regular expression language, a specialized language designed to do everything that was just discussed and much more. Like any language, regular expressions have a special syntax and instructions that you must learn.

> NOTE: **To Learn More**
>
> Full coverage of regular expressions is beyond the scope of this lesson. Although the basics are covered here, for a more thorough introduction to regular expressions, you might want to obtain a copy of my *Sams Teach Yourself Regular Expressions in 10 Minutes* (ISBN 0672325667).

Using Oracle PL/SQL Regular Expressions

So what does this have to do with Oracle? As already explained, all regular expressions do is match text, comparing a pattern (the regular expression) with a string of text. PL/SQL provides rather sophisticated support for regular expressions that you can use in `WHERE` clauses, allowing you to specify regular expressions that filter data retrieved using `SELECT`.

> NOTE: **Not Just in `WHERE` Clauses**
>
> PL/SQL provides four functions with which to access regular expressions. In this lesson, we focus only on using regular expressions to filter data, and so we only use the `REGEXP_LIKE()` function, and we do not use `REGEXP_REPLACE()` (used to replace characters in a string), or `REGEXP_INSTR()` and `REGEXP_SUBSTR()` (both used to perform searches for substrings within strings). The reason I point this out is so that you are aware that this additional functionality exists, because the regular expressions examples you'll learn while using `REGEXP_LIKE()` in this lesson also apply to those other functions.

This will all become much clearer with some examples.

Basic Character Matching

We'll start with a simple example. The following statement retrieves all rows where column `prod_name` contains the text `1000`:

Input ▼

```
SELECT prod_name
FROM products
WHERE REGEXP_LIKE(prod_name, '1000')
ORDER BY prod_name;
```

Output ▼

```
+--------------+
| prod_name    |
+--------------+
| JetPack 1000 |
+--------------+
```

Analysis ▼

This statement looks much like the ones that used `LIKE` (in Lesson 8, "Using Wildcard Filtering"), except that the `LIKE` has been replaced with a `REGEXP_LIKE()` function call. This tells Oracle to treat what follows as a regular expression (one that just matches the literal text `1000`).

> NOTE: **That's an Odd `WHERE` Clause**
>
> Before going further, let's take another look at the `WHERE` clause we just used. Every `WHERE` clause you've seen thus far required that you pass it a column name and a value, as well as an operator (`=`, or `LIKE`, for example). When Oracle processes the `WHERE` clauses, the result is either `true`, in which case the row is retrieved, or `false`, in which case it is not. `WHERE REGEXP_LIKE(prod_name, '1000')` is different; it's a function that takes parameters. So what is actually being checked? The answer is that `REGEXP_LIKE()` is indeed returning `true` or `false`, and when `true` (a match is found), that row matches the `WHERE` clause and is returned.

So, why bother using a regular expression? In the example just used, regular expressions really add no value (and probably hurt performance), but consider this next example:

Input ▼

```
SELECT prod_name
FROM products
WHERE REGEXP_LIKE(prod_name,  '.000')
ORDER BY prod_name;
```

Output ▼

```
+--------------+
| prod_name    |
+--------------+
| JetPack 1000 |
| JetPack 2000 |
+--------------+
```

Analysis ▼

Here the regular expression `.000` was used. `.` is a special character in the regular expression language. It means *match any single character*, and so both `1000` and `2000` matched and were returned.

Of course, this particular example could also have been accomplished using `LIKE` and wildcards (as discussed in Lesson 8).

> NOTE: `LIKE` **Versus** `REGEXP`
>
> There is one very important difference between `LIKE` and `REGEXP`. Look at these two statements:
>
> ```
> SELECT prod_name
> FROM products
> WHERE prod_name LIKE '1000'
> ORDER BY prod_name;
> ```
>
> and
>
> ```
> SELECT prod_name
> FROM products
> WHERE REGEXP_LIKE(prod_name, '1000')
> ORDER BY prod_name;
> ```
>
> If you were to try them both, you would discover that the first returns no data and the second returns one row. Why is this?

As shown in Lesson 8, `LIKE` matches an entire column. If the text to be matched existed in the middle of a column value, `LIKE` would not find it and the row would not be returned (unless wildcard characters were used). `REGEXP_LIKE()`, on the other hand, looks for matches within column values, and so if the text to be matched existed in the middle of a column value, `REGEXP_LIKE()` would find it and the row would be returned. This is a very important distinction.

So can `REGEXP_LIKE()` be used to match entire column values (so that it functions like `LIKE`)? Actually, yes, using the ^ and `$` anchors, as will be explained later in this lesson.

TIP: **Matches Are Case Sensitive**

Regular expression matching in Oracle is case sensitive.

Performing OR Matches

To search for one of two strings (either one or the other), use | as shown here:

Input ▼

```
SELECT prod_name
FROM products
WHERE REGEXP_LIKE(prod_name, '1000|2000')
ORDER BY prod_name;
```

Output ▼

```
+--------------+
| prod_name    |
+--------------+
| JetPack 1000 |
| JetPack 2000 |
+--------------+
```

Analysis ▼

Here the regular expression `1000|2000` was used. | is the regular expression OR operator. It means *match one or the other*, and so both `1000` and `2000` matched and were returned.

Using | is functionally similar to using OR statements in SELECT statements, with multiple OR conditions being consolidated into a single regular expression.

> TIP: **More Than Two** OR **Conditions**
>
> More than two OR conditions may be specified. For example, '1000|2000|3000' would match 1000 or 2000 or 3000.

Matching One of Several Characters

. matches any single character. But what if you wanted to match only specific characters? You can do this by specifying a set of characters enclosed within [and], as shown here:

Input ▼

```
SELECT prod_name
FROM products
WHERE REGEXP_LIKE(prod_name, '[123] ton')
ORDER BY prod_name;
```

Output ▼

```
+-------------+
| prod_name   |
+-------------+
| 1 ton anvil |
| 2 ton anvil |
+-------------+
```

Analysis ▼

Here the regular expression [123] ton was used. [123] defines a set of characters, and here it means *match* 1 *or* 2 *or* 3, so both 1 ton and 2 ton matched and were returned (there was no 3 ton).

As you have just seen, [] is another form of OR statement. In fact, the regular expression [123] Ton is shorthand for [1|2|3] ton, which also would have worked. But the [] characters are needed to define what the

OR statement is looking for. To better understand this, look at the next example:

Input ▼

```
SELECT prod_name
FROM products
WHERE REGEXP_LIKE(prod_name, '1|2|3 ton')
ORDER BY prod_name;
```

Output ▼

```
+---------------+
| prod_name     |
+---------------+
| 1 ton anvil   |
| 2 ton anvil   |
| JetPack 1000  |
| JetPack 2000  |
| TNT (1 stick) |
+---------------+
```

Analysis ▼

Well, that did not work. The two required rows were retrieved, but so were three others. This happened because Oracle assumed that you meant *'1' or '2' or '3 ton'*, and so any rows with product names containing `1` or `2` were also matched. The `|` character applies to the entire string unless it is enclosed with a set.

Sets of characters can also be negated. That is, they'll match anything *but* the specified characters. To negate a character set, place a ^ at the start of the set. So, whereas `[123]` matches characters `1`, `2`, or `3`, `[^123]` matches anything but those characters. Here's an example:

Input ▼

```
SELECT prod_name
FROM products
WHERE REGEXP_LIKE(prod_name, '[^123] ton')
ORDER BY prod_name;
```

Output ▼

```
+----------------+
| prod_name      |
+----------------+
| .5 ton anvil   |
+----------------+
```

Analysis ▼

`[^123]` means match anything other than the characters `1`, `2`, and `3`, and so `[^123] ton` matched the only other anvil.

Matching Ranges

Sets can be used to define one or more characters to be matched. For example, the following will match digits `0` through `9`:

```
[0123456789]
```

To simplify this type of set, `-` can be used to define a range. The following is functionally identical to the list of digits just shown:

```
[0-9]
```

Ranges are not limited to complete sets—`[1-3]` and `[6-9]` are valid ranges, too. In addition, ranges need not be numeric, and so `[a-z]` will match any alphabetical character.

Here is an example:

Input ▼

```
SELECT prod_name
FROM products
WHERE REGEXP_LIKE(prod_name, '[1-5] ton')
ORDER BY prod_name;
```

Output ▼

```
+--------------+
| prod_name    |
+--------------+
| .5 ton anvil |
| 1 ton anvil  |
| 2 ton anvil  |
+--------------+
```

Analysis ▼

Here the regular expression `[1-5] ton` was used. `[1-5]` defines a range, and so this expression means *match* `1` *through* `5`, and so three matches were returned. `.5 ton` was returned because `5 ton` matched (without the `.` character).

Matching Special Characters

The regular expression language is made up of special characters that have specific meanings. You've already seen `.`, `[]`, `|`, and `-`, and there are others, too. This begs the question: If you needed to match those characters, how would you do so? For example, if you wanted to find values that contain the `.` character, how would you search for it? Look at this example:

Input ▼

```
SELECT vend_name
FROM vendors
WHERE REGEXP_LIKE(vend_name, '.')
ORDER BY vend_name;
```

Output ▼

```
+----------------+
| vend_name      |
+----------------+
| ACME           |
| Anvils R Us    |
| Furball Inc.   |
| Jet Set        |
| Jouets Et Ours |
| LT Supplies    |
+----------------+
```

Analysis ▼

That did not work. . matches any character, and so every row was retrieved.

To match special characters, they must be preceded by \. So, \- means find - and \. means find .:

Input ▼

```
SELECT vend_name
FROM vendors
WHERE REGEXP_LIKE(vend_name, '\.')
ORDER BY vend_name;
```

Output ▼

```
+--------------+
| vend_name    |
+--------------+
| Furball Inc. |
+--------------+
```

Analysis ▼

That worked. \. matches ., and so only a single row was retrieved. This process is known as *escaping* (you saw that term used in the last lesson, too), and all characters that have special significance in regular expressions must be escaped this way. This includes ., |, [], and all the other special characters used thus far.

> TIP: **To Match **
>
> To match the backslash character itself (\), you need to escape it and use \\.

Matching Character Classes

There are matches that you'll find yourself using frequently, such as digits, or all alphabetical characters, or all alphanumerical characters, and so on. To make working with these easier, you can use predefined character sets known as *character classes*. Table 9.1 lists some of these character classes and what they mean.

TABLE 9.1 Character Classes

Class	Description
`\d`	Any digit (same as `[0-9]`)
`\D`	Any non-digit (same as `[^0-9]`)
`\w`	Any letter or digit (same as `[a-zA-Z0-9]`)
`\W`	Any non-letter or digit (same as `[^a-zA-Z0-9]`)
`\s`	Any white space character
`\S`	Any non-white space character

Matching Multiple Instances

All the regular expressions used thus far attempt to match a single occurrence. If there is a match, the row is retrieved, and if not, nothing is retrieved. But sometimes you'll require greater control over the number of matches. For example, you might want to locate all numbers regardless of how many digits the number contains, or you might want to locate a word but also be able to accommodate a trailing `s` if one exists, and so on.

This can be accomplished using the regular expressions repetition metacharacters, listed in Table 9.2.

TABLE 9.2 Repetition Metacharacters

Metacharacter	Description
`*`	0 or more matches
`+`	1 or more matches (equivalent to `{1,}`)
`?`	0 or 1 match (equivalent to `{0,1}`)
`{n}`	Specific number of matches
`{n,}`	No less than a specified number of matches
`{n,m}`	Range of matches

Following are some examples:

Input ▼

```
SELECT prod_name
FROM products
WHERE REGEXP_LIKE(prod_name, '\(\d sticks?\)')
ORDER BY prod_name;
```

Output ▼

```
+-----------------+
| prod_name       |
+-----------------+
| TNT (1 stick)   |
| TNT (5 sticks)  |
+-----------------+
```

Analysis ▼

Regular expression `'\(\d sticks?\)'` requires some explanation. `\(` matches `(`, `\d` matches any digit (`1` and `5` in this example), `sticks?` matches `stick` and `sticks` (the `?` after the `s` makes that `s` optional because `?` matches 0 or 1 occurrence of whatever it follows), and `\)` matches the closing `)`. Without `?`, it would have been very difficult to match both `stick` and `sticks`.

Here's another example. This time we'll try to match four consecutive digits:

Input ▼

```
SELECT prod_name
FROM products
WHERE REGEXP_LIKE(prod_name, '\d{4}')
ORDER BY prod_name;
```

Output ▼

```
+---------------+
| prod_name     |
+---------------+
| JetPack 1000  |
| JetPack 2000  |
+---------------+
```

Analysis ▼

As explained previously, `\d` matches any digit. `{4}` requires exactly four occurrences of whatever it follows (any digit), and so `\d{4}` matches any four consecutive digits.

It is worth noting that when you use regular expressions, there is almost always more than one way to write a specific expression. The previous example could have also been written as follows:

Input ▼

```
SELECT prod_name
FROM products
WHERE REGEXP_LIKE(prod_name, '[0-9][0-9][0-9][0-9]')
ORDER BY prod_name;
```

Actually, it could also have been written as:

Input ▼

```
SELECT prod_name
FROM products
WHERE REGEXP_LIKE(prod_name, '[0-9]{4}')
ORDER BY prod_name;
```

Anchors

All the examples thus far have matched text anywhere within a string. To match text at specific locations, you need to use anchors, as listed in Table 9.3.

TABLE 9.3 Anchor Metacharacters

Anchor	Description
^	Start of text
$	End of text

For example, what if you wanted to find all products that started with a number (including numbers starting with a decimal point)? A simple search for `[0-9\.]` (or `[\d\.]`) would not work because it would find matches anywhere within the text. The solution is to use the ^ anchor, as shown here:

Input ▼

```
SELECT prod_name
FROM products
WHERE REGEXP_LIKE(prod_name, '^[0-9\.]')
ORDER BY prod_name;
```

Output ▼

```
+--------------+
| prod_name    |
+--------------+
| .5 ton anvil |
| 1 ton anvil  |
| 2 ton anvil  |
+--------------+
```

Analysis ▼

^ matches the start of a string. As such, `^[0-9\.]` matches `.` or any digit only if they are the first characters within a string. Without the ^, four other rows would have been retrieved, too (those that have digits in the middle).

> NOTE: **The Dual Purpose ^**
>
> ^ has two uses. Within a set (defined using `[` and `]`), it is used to negate that set. Otherwise, it is used to refer to the starts of a string.

> NOTE: **Making `REGEXP_LIKE()` Behave Like `LIKE`**
>
> Earlier in this lesson, I mentioned that `LIKE` and `REGEXP_LIKE()` behaved differently in that `LIKE` matched an entire string and `REGEXP_LIKE()` matched substrings, too. Using anchors, `REGEXP_LIKE()` can be made to behave just like `LIKE` by simply starting each expression with ^ and ending it with `$`.

Summary

In this lesson, you learned the basics of regular expressions, and how to use them in Oracle PL/SQL `SELECT` statements via the `REGEXP_LIKE()` function.

Summary

LESSON 10
Creating Calculated Fields

In this lesson, you will learn what calculated fields are, how to create them, and how to use aliases to refer to them from within your application.

Understanding Calculated Fields

Data stored within a database's tables is often not available in the exact format needed by your applications. Here are some examples:

- You need to display a field containing the name of a company along with the company's location, but that information is stored in separated table columns.
- City, state, and ZIP Code are stored in separate columns (as they should be), but your mailing label printing program needs them retrieved as one correctly formatted field.
- Column data is in mixed upper- and lowercase, and your report needs all data presented in uppercase.
- An order items table stores item price and quantity but not the expanded price (price multiplied by quantity) of each item. To print invoices, you need that expanded price.
- You need total, averages, or other calculations based on table data.

In each of these examples, the data stored in the table is not exactly what your application needs. Rather than retrieve the data as it is and then reformat it within your client application or report, what you really want is to retrieve converted, calculated, or reformatted data directly from the database.

This is where calculated fields come in. Unlike all the columns we retrieved in the lessons thus far, calculated fields don't actually exist in database tables. Rather, a calculated field is created on the fly in a SQL `SELECT` statement.

> **Field** Essentially means the same thing as *column* and often is used interchangeably, although database columns are typically called *columns* and the term *fields* is normally used in conjunction with calculated fields.

It is important to note that only the database knows which columns in a `SELECT` statement are actual table columns and which are calculated fields. From the perspective of a client (for example, your application), a calculated field's data is returned in the same way as data from any other column.

> TIP: **Client Versus Server Formatting**
> Many of the conversions and reformatting that can be performed in SQL statements can also be performed directly in your client application. However, as a rule, it is far quicker to perform these operations on the database server than it is to perform them within the client because DBMSs are built to perform this type of processing quickly and efficiently.

Concatenating Fields

To demonstrate working with calculated fields, let's start with a simple example—creating a title made up of two columns.

The `vendors` table contains vendor name and address information. Imagine you are generating a vendor report and need to list the vendor location as part of the vendor name in the format `name (location)`.

The report wants a single value, and the data in the table is stored in two columns: `vend_name` and `vend_country`. In addition, you need to surround `vend_country` with parentheses, and those are definitely not stored in the database table. The `SELECT` statement that returns the vendor names and locations is simple enough, but how would you create this combined value?

> **Concatenate** Joining values together (by appending them to each other) to form a single long value.

The solution is to concatenate the two columns. In Oracle `SELECT` statements, you can concatenate columns using the || operator.

> TIP: **No + for Concatenation**
>
> Many DBMSs allow you to use + to concatenate strings. Oracle does not; you must use || for concatenation.

Input ▼

```
SELECT vend_name || ', (' || vend_country || ')'
FROM vendors
ORDER BY vend_name;
```

Output ▼

```
+-----------------------------------------------------+
| VEND_NAME||',('||VEND_COUNTRY||')'                  |
+-----------------------------------------------------+
| ACME                     , (USA                    )|
| Anvils R Us              , (USA                    )|
| Furball Inc.             , (USA                    )|
| Jet Set                  , (England                )|
| Jouets Et Ours           , (France                 )|
| LT Supplies              , (USA                    )|
+-----------------------------------------------------+
```

Analysis ▼

|| concatenates strings, appending them to each other to create one bigger string. The previous SELECT statements concatenate four elements:

- The name stored in the vend_name column
- A string containing a space and an open parenthesis
- The state stored in the vend_country column
- A string containing the close parenthesis

As you can see in the output shown previously, the SELECT statement returns a single column (a calculated field) containing all four of these elements as one unit. However, the output contains lots of extraneous spacing. What we really want is something like ACME, (USA).

Back in Lesson 8, "Using Wildcard Filtering," I mentioned the need to trim data to remove any trailing spaces. This can be done using the PL/SQL RTrim() function, as follows:

Input ▼

```
SELECT RTrim(vend_name) || ', (' || RTrim(vend_country) || ')'
FROM vendors
ORDER BY vend_name;
```

Output ▼

```
+-----------------------------------------------------+
| RTRIM(VEND_NAME)||',('||RTRIM(VEND_COUNTRY)||')'    |
+-----------------------------------------------------+
| ACME, (USA)                                         |
| Anvils R Us, (USA)                                  |
| Furball Inc., (USA)                                 |
| Jet Set, (England)                                  |
| Jouets Et Ours, (France)                            |
| LT Supplies, (USA)                                  |
+-----------------------------------------------------+
```

Analysis ▼

The `RTrim()` function trims all spaces from the right of a value. By using `RTrim()`, the individual columns are all trimmed properly.

> **The `Trim()` Functions** In addition to `RTrim()` (which, as just shown, trims the right side of a string), PL/SQL supports the use of `LTrim()` (which trims the left side of a string), and `Trim()` (which trims both the right and left).

Using Aliases

The `SELECT` statement used to concatenate the address field works well, as shown in the previous output. But what is the name of this new calculated column? Well, the truth is, it has no name; it is simply a value. Although this can be fine if you are just looking at the results in a SQL query tool, an unnamed column cannot be used within a client application because the client has no way to refer to that column.

To solve this problem, SQL supports column aliases. An *alias* is just that—an alternative name for a field or value. Aliases are assigned with the `AS` keyword. Take a look at the following `SELECT` statement:

Input ▼

```
SELECT RTrim(vend_name) || ', (' || RTrim(vend_country) || ')'
➥AS vend_title
FROM vendors
ORDER BY vend_name;
```

Output ▼

```
+-----------------------------------------------------+
| VEND_TITLE                                          |
+-----------------------------------------------------+
| ACME, (USA)                                         |
| Anvils R Us, (USA)                                  |
| Furball Inc., (USA)                                 |
| Jet Set, (England)                                  |
| Jouets Et Ours, (France)                            |
| LT Supplies, (USA)                                  |
+-----------------------------------------------------+
```

Analysis ▼

The SELECT statement itself is the same as the one used in the previous code snippet, except that here the calculated field is followed by the text `AS vend_title`. This instructs SQL to create a calculated field named `vend_title` containing the results of the specified calculation. As you can see in the output, the results are the same as before, but the column is now named `vend_title` and any client application can refer to this column by name, just as it would to any actual table column.

> TIP: **Other Uses for Aliases**
>
> Aliases have other uses, too. Some common uses include renaming a column if the real table column name contains illegal characters (for example, spaces) and expanding column names if the original names are either ambiguous or easily misread.

> NOTE: **Derived Columns**
>
> Aliases are also sometimes referred to as *derived columns*, so regardless of the term you run across, they mean the same thing.

Performing Mathematical Calculations

Another frequent use for calculated fields is performing mathematical calculations on retrieved data. Let's take a look at an example. The `orders` table contains all orders received, and the `orderitems` table contains the individual items in each order. The following SQL statement retrieves all the items in order number `20005`:

Input ▼

```
SELECT prod_id, quantity, item_price
FROM orderitems
WHERE order_num = 20005;
```

Output ▼

```
+---------+----------+------------+
| prod_id | quantity | item_price |
+---------+----------+------------+
| ANV01   |       10 |       5.99 |
| ANV02   |        3 |       9.99 |
| TNT2    |        5 |         10 |
| FB      |        1 |         10 |
+---------+----------+------------+
```

The `item_price` column contains the per unit price for each item in an order. To expand the item price (item price multiplied by quantity ordered), you simply do the following:

Input ▼

```
SELECT prod_id,
       quantity,
       item_price,
       quantity*item_price AS expanded_price
FROM orderitems
WHERE order_num = 20005;
```

Output ▼

```
+---------+----------+------------+----------------+
| prod_id | quantity | item_price | expanded_price |
+---------+----------+------------+----------------+
| ANV01   |       10 |       5.99 |           59.9 |
| ANV02   |        3 |       9.99 |          29.97 |
| TNT2    |        5 |         10 |             50 |
| FB      |        1 |         10 |             10 |
+---------+----------+------------+----------------+
```

Analysis ▼

The `expanded_price` column shown in the previous output is a calculated field; the calculation is simply `quantity*item_price`. The client application can now use this new calculated column just as it would any other column.

Oracle supports the basic mathematical operators listed in Table 10.1. In addition, parentheses can be used to establish order of precedence. Refer to Lesson 7, "Advanced Data Filtering," for an explanation of precedence.

TABLE 10.1 Oracle Mathematical Operators

Operator	Description
+	Addition
-	Subtraction
*	Multiplication
/	Division

> TIP: **How to Test Calculations**
>
> `SELECT` provides a great way to test and experiment with functions and calculations. Although `SELECT` is usually used to retrieve data from a table, the `FROM` clause can be omitted by replacing it with a special table named `dual`. For example, `SELECT 3 * 2 FROM dual;` would return `6`, and `SELECT Trim(' abc ') FROM dual;` would return `abc`. If that `dual` table looks vaguely familiar, it's because we used it in our first PL/SQL statement back in Lesson 3, "Working with Oracle."

Summary

In this lesson, you learned what calculated fields are and how to create them. We used examples demonstrating the use of calculated fields for both string concatenation and mathematical operations. In addition, you learned how to create and use aliases so your application can refer to calculated fields.

LESSON 11

Using Data Manipulation Functions

In this lesson, you'll learn what functions are, what types of functions Oracle supports, and how to use these functions.

Understanding Functions

Like almost any other computer language, SQL supports the use of functions to manipulate data. Functions are operations that are usually performed on data, usually to facilitate conversion and manipulation.

An example of a function is the `RTrim()` that we used in the last lesson to trim any spaces from the end of a string.

> NOTE: **Functions Are Less Portable Than SQL**
>
> Code that runs on multiple systems is said to be *portable*. Most SQL statements are relatively portable, and when differences between SQL implementations do occur, they are usually not that difficult to deal with. Functions, on the other hand, tend to be far less portable. Just about every major DBMS supports functions that others don't, and sometimes the differences are significant.
>
> With code portability in mind, many SQL programmers opt not to use any implementation-specific features. Although this is a somewhat noble and idealistic view, it is not always in the best interests of application performance. If you opt not to use these functions, you make your application code work harder. It must use other methods to do what the DBMS could have done more efficiently.
>
> If you do decide to use functions, make sure you comment your code well, so that at a later date, you (or another developer) will know exactly to which SQL implementation you were writing. Code commenting was introduced back in Lesson 4, "Retrieving Data."

Using Functions

Most SQL implementations support the following types of functions:

- Text functions are used to manipulate strings of text (for example, trimming or padding values and converting values to upper- and lowercase).
- Numeric functions are used to perform mathematical operations on numeric data (for example, returning absolute numbers and performing algebraic calculations).
- Date and time functions are used to manipulate date and time values and to extract specific components from these values (for example, returning differences between dates and checking date validity).
- System functions return information specific to the DBMS being used (for example, returning user login information or checking version specifics).

Text Manipulation Functions

You've already seen an example of text-manipulation functions in the last lesson—the `RTrim()` function was used to trim white space from the end of a column value. Here is another example, this time using the `Upper()` function:

Input ▼

```
SELECT vend_name, Upper(vend_name) AS vend_name_upcase
FROM vendors
ORDER BY vend_name;
```

Output ▼

```
+----------------+------------------+
| vend_name      | vend_name_upcase |
+----------------+------------------+
| ACME           | ACME             |
| Anvils R Us    | ANVILS R US      |
| Furball Inc.   | FURBALL INC.     |
| Jet Set        | JET SET          |
```

```
| Jouets Et Ours | JOUETS ET OURS   |
| LT Supplies    | LT SUPPLIES      |
+----------------+------------------+
```

Analysis ▼

As you can see, `Upper()` converts text to uppercase, and so in this example, each vendor is listed twice, first exactly as stored in the `vendors` table, and then converted to uppercase as column `vend_name_upcase`.

Table 11.1 lists some commonly used text-manipulation functions.

TABLE 11.1 Commonly Used Text-Manipulation Functions

Function	Description
`Length()`	Returns the length of a string
`Lower()`	Converts string to lowercase
`LPad()`	Pads spaces to left of string
`LTrim()`	Trims white space from left of string
`RPad()`	Pads spaces to right of string
`RTrim()`	Trims white space from right of string
`Soundex()`	Returns a string's SOUNDEX value
`SubString()`	Returns characters from within a string
`Upper()`	Converts string to uppercase

One item in Table 11.1 requires further explanation. SOUNDEX is an algorithm that converts any string of text into an alphanumeric pattern describing the phonetic representation of that text. SOUNDEX takes into account similar sounding characters and syllables, enabling strings to be compared by how they sound rather than how they have been typed. Although SOUNDEX is not a SQL concept, Oracle (like many other DBMSs) offers SOUNDEX support.

Here's an example using the `Soundex()` function. Customer `Coyote Inc.` is in the `customers` table and has a contact named `Y. Lee`. But what if that were a typo, and the contact actually was supposed to have been `Y. Lie`? Obviously, searching by the correct contact name would return no data, as shown here:

Input ▼

```
SELECT cust_name, cust_contact
FROM customers
WHERE cust_contact = 'Y. Lie';
```

Output ▼

```
+-------------+--------------+
| cust_name   | cust_contact |
+-------------+--------------+
```

Now try the same search using the `Soundex()` function to match all contact names that sound similar to `Y. Lie`:

Input ▼

```
SELECT cust_name, cust_contact
FROM customers
WHERE Soundex(cust_contact) = Soundex('Y Lie');
```

Output ▼

```
+-------------+--------------+
| cust_name   | cust_contact |
+-------------+--------------+
| Coyote Inc. | Y Lee        |
+-------------+--------------+
```

Analysis ▼

In this example, the `WHERE` clause uses the `Soundex()` function to convert both the `cust_contact` column value and the search string to their SOUNDEX values. Because `Y. Lee` and `Y. Lie` sound alike, their SOUNDEX values match, and so the `WHERE` clause correctly filtered the desired data.

Date and Time Manipulation Functions

Date and times are stored in tables using special datatypes using special internal formats so they may be sorted or filtered quickly and efficiently, as well as to save physical storage space.

The format used to store dates and times is usually of no use to your applications, and so date and time functions are almost always used to read, expand, and manipulate these values. Because of this, date and time manipulation functions are some of the most important functions in Oracle PL/SQL.

Table 11.2 lists some commonly used date and time manipulation functions.

TABLE 11.2 Commonly Used Date and Time Manipulation Functions

Function	Description
`Add_Month()`	Adds months to a date (can also subtract)
`Extract()`	Extracts year, month, day, hour, minute, or second from a date and time
`Last_Day()`	Returns the last day of a month
`Months_Between()`	Returns the number of months between two months
`Next_Day()`	Returns the day after a specified date
`Sysdate()`	Returns the current date and time
`To_Date()`	Converts a string to a date

> NOTE: **The All-Important `Extract()` Function**
>
> If you've used other DBMSs, you're probably wondering why PL/SQL has so few date and time functions. Other DBMSs have far more, including shortcuts for extracting specific values from dates and times. In PL/SQL, one function does it all—the all-important `Extract()` function—as you will soon see.

This would be a good time to revisit data filtering using `WHERE`. Thus far we have filtered data using `WHERE` clauses that compared numbers and text, but frequently data needs to be filtered by date. Filtering by date requires some extra care, and the use of special PL/SQL functions.

The first thing to keep in mind is the date formatting can get tricky. After all, what date is `2015-03-04`? Is `03` the month and `04` the day, or vice versa? For this reason, any time you provide a date to Oracle, you must explicitly state how it is formatted.

> TIP: **Always Use Four-Digit Years**
>
> Oracle uses four-digit years. If you provide a two-digit year, Oracle might not treat it as you would expect. As such, it is far safer to always use a full four-digit year so that Oracle does not have to make any assumptions for you.

As such, a basic date comparison should be simple enough:

Input ▼

```
SELECT cust_id, order_num
FROM orders
WHERE order_date = TO_DATE('2015-02-01', 'yyyy-mm-dd');
```

Output ▼

```
+---------+-----------+
| cust_id | order_num |
+---------+-----------+
|   10001 |     20005 |
+---------+-----------+
```

Analysis ▼

That `SELECT` statement worked; it retrieved a single order record, one with an `order_date` of `2015-02-01`. To prevent ambiguity, the `To_Date()` function was passed a formatting string of `yyyy-mm-dd`, which tells Oracle that the date is formatted as a four-digit year, followed by a hyphen, followed by a two-digit month, followed by another hyphen, and then a two-digit date.

Another thing to keep in mind is that our `order_date` field is indeed a date field, not a date and time field. I did this to simplify things, but in the real world, order may indeed be saved with order date and order time. Had `order_date` been a datetime field, things would have gotten a bit more complicated. Why? Because `WHERE order_date = TO_DATE('2015-02-01', 'yyyy-mm-dd');` would fail if, for example, the stored `order_date` value was `2015-02-01 11:30:05`. Even though a row with that date is present, it would not be retrieved because the `WHERE` match failed.

The solution in this case would be to instruct Oracle to search a date range, like this:

Input ▼

```
SELECT cust_id, order_num
FROM orders
WHERE order_date >= TO_DATE('2015-02-01', 'yyyy-mm-dd')
   AND order_date < TO_DATE('2015-02-02', 'yyyy-mm-dd')
```

This same technique can be used to search for date ranges. For example, what if you wanted to retrieve all orders placed in February 2015? There are several solutions, one of which is similar to the preceding:

Input ▼

```
SELECT cust_id, order_num
FROM orders
WHERE order_date >= TO_DATE('2015-02-01', 'yyyy-mm-dd')
   AND order_date < TO_DATE('2015-03-01', 'yyyy-mm-dd');
```

Output ▼

```
+---------+-----------+
| cust_id | order_num |
+---------+-----------+
|   10001 |     20005 |
|   10003 |     20006 |
|   10004 |     20007 |
+---------+-----------+
```

You could also use the `BETWEEN` operator, discussed in Lesson 6, "Filtering Data."

Input ▼

```
SELECT cust_id, order_num
FROM orders
WHERE order_date BETWEEN TO_DATE('2015-02-01', 'yyyy-mm-dd')
   AND TO_DATE('2015-02-28', 'yyyy-mm-dd');
```

Analysis ▼

Here a `BETWEEN` operator is used to define `2015-02-01` and `2015-02-28` as the range of dates to match.

More flexible date arithmetic requires the ability to extract specific parts of a date or time. This is where the `Extract()` function comes into play. As its name suggests, `Extract()` extracts parts of dates and times, allowing you to work with just the `YEAR`, `MONTH`, `DAY`, `HOUR`, `MINUTE`, and `SECOND`.

Here's another solution to the previous problem (one that won't require you to figure out how many days are in each month, or worry about February in leap years):

Input ▼

```
SELECT cust_id, order_num
FROM orders
WHERE Extract(Year FROM order_date) = 2015
   AND Extract(Month FROM order_date) = 2
```

Output ▼

```
+---------+-----------+
| cust_id | order_num |
+---------+-----------+
|   10001 |     20005 |
|   10003 |     20006 |
|   10004 |     20007 |
+---------+-----------+
```

Analysis ▼

`Extract(Year)` returns the year from a date. Similarly, `Extract(Month)` returns the month from a date. `WHERE Extract(Year FROM order_date) = 2015 AND Extract(Month FROM order_date) = 2` thus retrieves all rows that have an `order_date` in year `2015` and in month `2`.

Numeric Manipulation Functions

Numeric manipulation functions do just that—manipulate numeric data. These functions tend to be used primarily for algebraic, trigonometric, or geometric calculations and, therefore, are not as frequently used as string or date and time manipulation functions.

The ironic thing is that of all the functions found in the major DBMSs, the numeric functions are the ones that are most uniform and consistent. Table 11.3 lists some of the more commonly used numeric manipulation functions.

TABLE 11.3 Commonly Used Numeric Manipulation Functions

Function	Description
`Abs()`	Returns a number's absolute value
`Cos()`	Returns the trigonometric cosine of a specified angle
`Exp()`	Returns the exponential value of a specific number
`Mod()`	Returns the remainder of a division operation
`Sin()`	Returns the trigonometric sine of a specified angle
`Sqrt()`	Returns the square root of a specified number
`Tan()`	Returns the trigonometric tangent of a specified angle

Summary

In this lesson, you learned how to use SQL's data manipulation functions, and paid special attention to working with dates.

LESSON 12

Summarizing Data

In this lesson, you will learn what the SQL aggregate functions are and how to use them to summarize table data.

Using Aggregate Functions

It is often necessary to summarize data without actually retrieving it all, and Oracle provides special functions for this purpose. Using these functions, Oracle queries are often used to retrieve data for analysis and reporting purposes. Examples of this type of retrieval include the following:

- Determining the number of rows in a table (or the number of rows that meet some condition or contain a specific value)
- Obtaining the sum of a group of rows in a table
- Finding the highest, lowest, and average values in a table column (either for all rows or for specific rows)

In each of these examples, you want a summary of the data in a table, not the actual data itself. Therefore, returning the actual table data would be a waste of time and processing resources (not to mention bandwidth). To repeat, all you really want is the summary information.

To facilitate this type of retrieval, Oracle features a set of aggregate functions, some of which are listed in Table 12.1. These functions enable you to perform all the types of retrieval just enumerated.

> **Aggregate Functions** Functions that operate on a set of rows to calculate and return a single value.

TABLE 12.1 SQL Aggregate Functions

Function	Description
`AVG()`	Returns a column's average value
`COUNT()`	Returns the number of rows in a column
`MAX()`	Returns a column's highest value
`MIN()`	Returns a column's lowest value
`SUM()`	Returns the sum of a column's values

The use of each of these functions is explained in the following sections.

> NOTE: **Standard Deviation**
>
> A series of standard deviation aggregate functions are also supported by Oracle, but are not covered in the lessons.

The `AVG()` Function

`AVG()` is used to return the average value of a specific column by counting both the number of rows in the table and the sum of their values. `AVG()` can be used to return the average value of all columns or of specific columns or rows.

This first example uses `AVG()` to return the average price of all the products in the `products` table:

Input ▼

```
SELECT AVG(prod_price) AS avg_price
FROM products;
```

Output ▼

```
+------------+
| avg_price  |
+------------+
| 16.1335714 |
+------------+
```

Analysis ▼

The preceding SELECT statement returns a single value, avg_price, that contains the average price of all products in the products table. avg_price is an alias, as explained in Lesson 10, "Creating Calculated Fields."

AVG() can also be used to determine the average value of specific columns or rows. The following example returns the average price of products offered by a specific vendor:

Input ▼

```
SELECT AVG(prod_price) AS avg_price
FROM products
WHERE vend_id = 1003;
```

Output ▼

```
+-----------+
| avg_price  |
+------------+
| 13.2128571 |
+------------+
```

Analysis ▼

This SELECT statement differs from the previous one only in that this one contains a WHERE clause. The WHERE clause filters only products with a vend_id of 1003, and, therefore, the value returned in avg_price is the average of just that vendor's products.

> CAUTION: **Individual Columns Only**
>
> AVG() may only be used to determine the average of a specific numeric column, and that column name must be specified as the function parameter. To obtain the average value of multiple columns, multiple AVG() functions must be used.

> NOTE: NULL **Values**
>
> Column rows containing NULL values are ignored by the AVG() function.

The COUNT() Function

COUNT() does just that: It counts. Using COUNT(), you can determine the number of rows in a table or the number of rows that match a specific criterion.

COUNT() can be used two ways:

- Use COUNT(*) to count the number of rows in a table, whether columns contain values or NULL values.
- Use COUNT(column) to count the number of rows that have values in a specific column, ignoring NULL values.

This first example returns the total number of customers in the customers table:

Input ▼

```
SELECT COUNT(*) AS num_cust
FROM customers;
```

Output ▼

```
+----------+
| num_cust |
+----------+
|        5 |
+----------+
```

Analysis ▼

In this example, COUNT(*) is used to count all rows, regardless of values. The count is returned in num_cust.

The following example counts just the customers with an email address:

Input ▼

```
SELECT COUNT(cust_email) AS num_cust
FROM customers;
```

Output ▼

```
+-----------+
| num_cust  |
+-----------+
|         3 |
+-----------+
```

Analysis ▼

This SELECT statement uses COUNT(cust_email) to count only rows with a value in the cust_email column. In this example, cust_email is 3 (meaning that only three of the five customers have email addresses).

> NOTE: NULL **Values**
>
> Column rows with NULL values in them are ignored by the COUNT() function if a column name is specified, but not if the asterisk (*) is used.

The MAX() Function

MAX() returns the highest value in a specified column. MAX() requires that the column name be specified, as shown here:

Input ▼

```
SELECT MAX(prod_price) AS max_price
FROM products;
```

Output ▼

```
+-----------+
| max_price |
+-----------+
|        55 |
+-----------+
```

Analysis ▼

Here MAX() returns the price of the most expensive item in the products table.

> TIP: **Using MAX() with Non-Numeric Data**
>
> Although MAX() is usually used to find the highest numeric or date values, Oracle allows it to be used to return the highest value in any column including textual columns. When used with textual data, MAX() returns the row that would be the last if the data were sorted by that column.

> NOTE: NULL **Values**
>
> Column rows with NULL values in them are ignored by the MAX() function.

The MIN() Function

MIN() does the exact opposite of MAX(); it returns the lowest value in a specified column. Like MAX(), MIN() requires that the column name be specified, as shown here:

Input ▼

```
SELECT MIN(prod_price) AS min_price
FROM products;
```

Output ▼

```
+-----------+
| min_price |
+-----------+
|       2.5 |
+-----------+
```

Analysis ▼

Here MIN() returns the price of the least expensive item in the products table.

> TIP: **Using `MIN()` with Non-Numeric Data**
>
> As with the `MAX()` function, Oracle allows `MIN()` to be used to return the lowest value in any columns including textual columns. When used with textual data, `MIN()` returns the row that would be first if the data were sorted by that column.

> NOTE: **`NULL` Values**
>
> Column rows with `NULL` values in them are ignored by the `MIN()` function.

The `SUM()` Function

`SUM()` is used to return the sum (total) of the values in a specific column.

Here is an example to demonstrate this. The `orderitems` table contains the actual items in an order, and each item has an associated `quantity`. The total number of items ordered (the sum of all the `quantity` values) can be retrieved as follows:

Input ▼

```
SELECT SUM(quantity) AS items_ordered
FROM orderitems
WHERE order_num = 20005;
```

Output ▼

```
+---------------+
| items_ordered |
+---------------+
|            19 |
+---------------+
```

Analysis ▼

The function `SUM(quantity)` returns the sum of all the item quantities in an order, and the `WHERE` clause ensures that just the right order items are included.

`SUM()` can also be used to total calculated values. In this next example, the total order amount is retrieved by totaling `item_price*quantity` for each item:

Input ▼

```
SELECT SUM(item_price*quantity) AS total_price
FROM orderitems
WHERE order_num = 20005;
```

Output ▼

```
+-------------+
| total_price |
+-------------+
|      149.87 |
+-------------+
```

Analysis ▼

The function `SUM(item_price*quantity)` returns the sum of all the expanded prices in an order, and again the `WHERE` clause ensures that just the correct order items are included.

> TIP: **Performing Calculations on Multiple Columns**
>
> All the aggregate functions can be used to perform calculations on multiple columns using the standard mathematical operators, as shown in the example.

> NOTE: `NULL` **Values**
>
> Column rows with `NULL` values in them are ignored by the `SUM()` function.

Aggregates on Distinct Values

The five aggregate functions can all be used in two ways:

- To perform calculations on all rows, specify the ALL argument, or specify no argument at all (because ALL is the default behavior).
- To only include unique values, specify the DISTINCT argument.

> TIP: ALL **Is Default**
>
> The ALL argument need not be specified because it is the default behavior. If DISTINCT is not specified, ALL is assumed.

The following example uses the AVG() function to return the average product price offered by a specific vendor. It is the same SELECT statement used in the previous example, but here the DISTINCT argument is used so the average only takes into account unique prices:

Input ▼

```
SELECT AVG(DISTINCT prod_price) AS avg_price
FROM products
WHERE vend_id = 1003;
```

Output ▼

```
+-----------+
| avg_price |
+-----------+
|    15.998 |
+-----------+
```

Analysis ▼

As you can see, in this example, avg_price is higher when DISTINCT is used because there are multiple items with the same lower price. Excluding them raises the average price.

> CAUTION: **Using** `DISTINCT`
>
> `DISTINCT` may only be used with `COUNT()` if a column name is specified. `DISTINCT` may not be used with `COUNT(*)`, and so `COUNT(DISTINCT *)` is not allowed and generates an error. Similarly, `DISTINCT` must be used with a column name and not with a calculation or expression.

> TIP: **Using** `DISTINCT` **with** `MIN()` **and** `MAX()`
>
> Although `DISTINCT` can technically be used with `MIN()` and `MAX()`, there is actually no value in doing so. The minimum and maximum values in a column are the same whether or not only distinct values are included.

Combining Aggregate Functions

All the examples of aggregate functions used thus far have involved a single function. But actually, `SELECT` statements may contain as few or as many aggregate functions as needed. Look at this example:

Input ▼

```
SELECT COUNT(*) AS num_items,
       MIN(prod_price) AS price_min,
       MAX(prod_price) AS price_max,
       AVG(prod_price) AS price_avg
FROM products;
```

Output ▼

```
+-----------+-----------+-----------+------------+
| num_items | price_min | price_max | price_avg  |
+-----------+-----------+-----------+------------+
|        14 |       2.5 |        55 | 16.1335714 |
+-----------+-----------+-----------+------------+
```

Analysis ▼

Here a single `SELECT` statement performs four aggregate calculations in one step and returns four values (the number of items in the `products` table; and the highest, lowest, and average product prices).

> TIP: **Naming Aliases**
>
> When specifying alias names to contain the results of an aggregate function, try to not use the name of an actual column in the table. Although there is nothing actually illegal about doing so, using unique names makes your SQL easier to understand and work with (and troubleshoot in the future).

Summary

Aggregate functions are used to summarize data. Oracle supports a range of aggregate functions, all of which can be used in multiple ways to return just the results you need. These functions are designed to be highly efficient, and they usually return results far more quickly than you could calculate them yourself in your own client application.

LESSON 13

Grouping Data

In this lesson, you'll learn how to group data so you can summarize subsets of table contents. This involves two new `SELECT` statement clauses: the `GROUP BY` clause and the `HAVING` clause.

Understanding Data Grouping

In the last lesson, you learned that the SQL aggregate functions can be used to summarize data. This enables you to count rows, calculate sums and averages, and obtain high and low values without having to retrieve all the data.

All the calculations thus far were performed on all the data in a table or on data that matched a specific `WHERE` clause. As a reminder, the following example returns the number of products offered by vendor `1003`:

Input ▼

```
SELECT COUNT(*) AS num_prods
FROM products
WHERE vend_id = 1003;
```

Output ▼

```
+-----------+
| num_prods |
+-----------+
|         7 |
+-----------+
```

But what if you want to return the number of products offered by each vendor? Or products offered by vendors who offer a single product, or only those who offer more than 10 products?

This is where groups come into play. Grouping enables you to divide data into logical sets so you can perform aggregate calculations on each group.

Creating Groups

Groups are created using the `GROUP BY` clause in your `SELECT` statement. The best way to understand this is to look at an example:

Input ▼

```
SELECT vend_id, COUNT(*) AS num_prods
FROM products
GROUP BY vend_id;
```

Output ▼

```
+---------+-----------+
| vend_id | num_prods |
+---------+-----------+
|    1001 |         3 |
|    1002 |         2 |
|    1003 |         7 |
|    1005 |         2 |
+---------+-----------+
```

Analysis ▼

The preceding `SELECT` statement specifies two columns: `vend_id`, which contains the ID of a product's vendor, and `num_prods`, which is a calculated field (created using the `COUNT(*)` function). The `GROUP BY` clause instructs Oracle to sort the data and group it by `vend_id`. This causes `num_prods` to be calculated once per `vend_id` rather than once for the entire table. As you can see in the output, vendor `1001` has `3` products listed, vendor `1002` has `2` products listed, vendor `1003` has `7` products listed, and vendor `1005` has `2` products listed.

Because you used GROUP BY, you did not have to specify each group to be evaluated and calculated. That was done automatically. The GROUP BY clause instructs Oracle to group the data and then perform the aggregate on each group rather than on the entire result set.

Before you use GROUP BY, here are some important rules about its use that you need to know:

- GROUP BY clauses can contain as many columns as you want. This enables you to nest groups, providing you with more granular control over how data is grouped.
- If you have nested groups in your GROUP BY clause, data is summarized at the last specified group. In other words, all the columns specified are evaluated together when grouping is established (so you won't get data back for each individual column level).
- Every column listed in GROUP BY must be a retrieved column or a valid expression (but not an aggregate function). If an expression is used in the SELECT, that same expression must be specified in GROUP BY. Aliases cannot be used.
- Aside from the aggregate calculations statements, every column in your SELECT statement should be present in the GROUP BY clause.
- If the grouping column contains a row with a NULL value, NULL will be returned as a group. If there are multiple rows with NULL values, they'll all be grouped together.
- The GROUP BY clause must come after any WHERE clause and before any ORDER BY clause.

Filtering Groups

In addition to being able to group data using GROUP BY, Oracle also allows you to filter which groups to include and which to exclude. For example, you might want a list of all customers who have made at least two orders. To obtain this data, you must filter based on the complete group, not on individual rows.

You've already seen the WHERE clause in action (introduced back in Lesson 6, "Filtering Data"). But WHERE does not work here because WHERE filters specific rows, not groups. As a matter of fact, WHERE has no idea what a group is.

So what do you use instead of WHERE? Oracle provides yet another clause for this purpose: the HAVING clause. HAVING is very similar to WHERE. In fact, all types of WHERE clauses you learned about thus far can also be used with HAVING. The only difference is that WHERE filters rows and HAVING filters groups.

> TIP: HAVING **Supports All of** WHERE**'s Operators**
>
> In Lesson 6 and Lesson 7, "Advanced Data Filtering," you learned about WHERE clause conditions (including wildcard conditions and clauses with multiple operators). All the techniques and options you learned about WHERE can be applied to HAVING. The syntax is identical; just the keyword is different.

So how do you filter rows? Look at the following example:

Input ▼

```
SELECT cust_id, COUNT(*) AS orders
FROM orders
GROUP BY cust_id
HAVING COUNT(*) >= 2;
```

Output ▼

```
+---------+--------+
| cust_id | orders |
+---------+--------+
|   10001 |      2 |
+---------+--------+
```

Analysis ▼

The first three lines of this SELECT statement are similar to the statements shown previously. The final line adds a HAVING clause that filters on those groups with a COUNT(*) >= 2—two or more orders.

Obviously, a WHERE clause couldn't have worked here because the filtering is based on the group aggregate value, not on the values of specific rows.

> NOTE: **The Difference Between HAVING and WHERE**
>
> Here's another way to look at it: WHERE filters before data is grouped, and HAVING filters after data is grouped. This is an important distinction; rows that are eliminated by a WHERE clause are not included in the group. This could change the calculated values, which in turn could affect which groups are filtered based on the use of those values in the HAVING clause.

So is there ever a need to use both WHERE and HAVING clauses in one statement? Actually, yes, there is. Suppose you want to further filter the previous statement so it returns any customers who placed two or more orders in the past 12 months. To do that, you can add a WHERE clause that filters out just the orders placed in the past 12 months. You then add a HAVING clause to filter just the groups with two or more rows in them.

To better demonstrate this, look at the following example that lists all vendors who have 2 or more products priced at 10 or more:

Input ▼

```
SELECT vend_id, COUNT(*) AS num_prods
FROM products
WHERE prod_price >= 10
GROUP BY vend_id
HAVING COUNT(*) >= 2;
```

Output ▼

```
+---------+-----------+
| vend_id | num_prods |
+---------+-----------+
|    1003 |         4 |
|    1005 |         2 |
+---------+-----------+
```

Analysis ▼

This statement warrants an explanation. The first line is a basic SELECT using an aggregate function—much like the examples thus far. The WHERE clause filters all rows with a prod_price of at least 10. Data is then grouped by vend_id, and then a HAVING clause filters just those groups with a count of 2 or more. Without the WHERE clause, two extra rows would have been retrieved (vendor 1002 who only sells products all priced under 10, and vendor 1001 who sells three products but only one of them is priced greater or equal to 10), as shown here:

Input ▼

```
SELECT vend_id, COUNT(*) AS num_prods
FROM products
GROUP BY vend_id
HAVING COUNT(*) >= 2;
```

Output ▼

```
+---------+-----------+
| vend_id | num_prods |
+---------+-----------+
|    1001 |         3 |
|    1002 |         2 |
|    1003 |         7 |
|    1005 |         2 |
+---------+-----------+
```

Grouping and Sorting

It is important to understand that GROUP BY and ORDER BY are very different, even though they often accomplish the same thing. Table 13.1 summarizes the differences between them.

TABLE 13.1 ORDER BY Versus GROUP BY

ORDER BY	GROUP BY
Sorts generated output.	Groups rows. The output might not be in group order, however.
Any columns (even columns not selected) may be used.	Only selected columns or expressions columns may be used, and every selected column expression must be used.
Never required.	Required if using columns (or expressions) with aggregate functions.

The first difference listed in Table 13.1 is extremely important. More often than not, you will find that data grouped using GROUP BY will indeed be output in group order. But that is not always the case, and it is not actually required by the SQL specifications. Furthermore, you might actually want it sorted differently than it is grouped. Just because you group data one way (to obtain group-specific aggregate values) does not mean that you want the output sorted that same way. You should always provide an explicit ORDER BY clause as well, even if it is identical to the GROUP BY clause.

> TIP: **Don't Forget** ORDER BY
>
> As a rule, any time you use a GROUP BY clause, you should also specify an ORDER BY clause. That is the only way to ensure that data is sorted properly. Never rely on GROUP BY to sort your data.

To demonstrate the use of both GROUP BY and ORDER BY, let's look at an example. The following SELECT statement is similar to the ones shown previously. It retrieves the order number and total order price of all orders with a total price of 50 or more:

Input ▼

```
SELECT order_num, SUM(quantity*item_price) AS ordertotal
FROM orderitems
GROUP BY order_num
HAVING SUM(quantity*item_price) >= 50;
```

Output ▼

```
+-----------+------------+
| order_num | ordertotal |
+-----------+------------+
|     20005 |     149.87 |
|     20006 |         55 |
|     20007 |       1000 |
|     20008 |        125 |
+-----------+------------+
```

To sort the output by order total, all you need to do is add an `ORDER BY` clause, as follows:

Input ▼

```
SELECT order_num, SUM(quantity*item_price) AS ordertotal
FROM orderitems
GROUP BY order_num
HAVING SUM(quantity*item_price) >= 50
ORDER BY ordertotal;
```

Output ▼

```
+-----------+------------+
| order_num | ordertotal |
+-----------+------------+
|     20006 |         55 |
|     20008 |        125 |
|     20005 |     149.87 |
|     20007 |       1000 |
+-----------+------------+
```

Analysis ▼

In this example, the `GROUP BY` clause is used to group the data by order number (the `order_num` column) so that the `SUM(*)` function can return the total order price. The `HAVING` clause filters the data so that only orders with a total price of `50` or more are returned. Finally, the output is sorted using the `ORDER BY` clause.

SELECT **Clause Ordering**

This is probably a good time to review the order in which SELECT statement clauses are to be specified. Table 13.2 lists all the clauses you have learned thus far, in the order they must be used.

TABLE 13.2 SELECT Clauses and Their Sequence

Clause	Description	Required
SELECT	Columns or expressions to be returned	Yes
FROM	Table to retrieve data from	Yes (in Oracle; no in most other DBMSs)
WHERE	Row-level filtering	No
GROUP BY	Group specification	Only if calculating aggregates by group
HAVING	Group-level filtering	No
ORDER BY	Output sort order	No

Summary

In Lesson 12, "Summarizing Data," you learned how to use the SQL aggregate functions to perform summary calculations on your data. In this lesson, you learned how to use the GROUP BY clause to perform these calculations on groups of data, returning results for each group. You saw how to use the HAVING clause to filter specific groups. You also learned the difference between ORDER BY and GROUP BY and between WHERE and HAVING.

LESSON 14

Working with Subqueries

In this lesson, you'll learn what subqueries are and how to use them.

Understanding Subqueries

`SELECT` statements are SQL queries. All the `SELECT` statements you have seen thus far are simple queries: single statements retrieving data from individual database tables.

> **Query** Any SQL statement. However, the term is usually used to refer to `SELECT` statements.

SQL also enables you to create *subqueries*: queries that are embedded into other queries. Why would you want to do this? The best way to understand this concept is to look at a couple of examples.

Filtering by Subquery

The database tables used in all the lessons in this book are relational tables. (See Appendix A, "The Example Tables," for a description of each of the tables and their relationships.) Order data is stored in two tables. The `orders` table stores a single row for each order containing order number, customer ID, and order date. The individual order items are stored in the related `orderitems` table. The `orders` table does not store customer information. It only stores a customer ID. The actual customer information is stored in the `customers` table.

Now suppose you wanted a list of all the customers who ordered item `TNT2`. What would you have to do to retrieve this information? Here are the steps:

1. Retrieve the order numbers of all orders containing item `TNT2`.
2. Retrieve the customer ID of all the customers who have orders listed in the order numbers returned in the previous step.
3. Retrieve the customer information for all the customer IDs returned in the previous step.

Each of these steps can be executed as a separate query. By doing so, you use the results returned by one `SELECT` statement to populate the `WHERE` clause of the next `SELECT` statement.

You can also use subqueries to combine all three queries into one single statement.

The first `SELECT` statement should be self-explanatory by now. It retrieves the `order_num` column for all order items with a `prod_id` of `TNT2`. The output lists the two orders containing this item:

Input ▼

```
SELECT order_num
FROM orderitems
WHERE prod_id = 'TNT2';
```

Output ▼

```
+-----------+
| order_num |
+-----------+
|     20005 |
|     20007 |
+-----------+
```

The next step is to retrieve the customer IDs associated with orders `20005` and `20007`. Using the `IN` clause described in Lesson 7, "Advanced Data Filtering," you can create a `SELECT` statement as follows:

Input ▼

```
SELECT cust_id
FROM orders
WHERE order_num IN (20005,20007);
```

Output ▼

```
+---------+
| cust_id |
+---------+
|   10001|
|   10004 |
+---------+
```

Now, combine the two queries by turning the first (the one that returned the order numbers) into a subquery. Look at the following SELECT statement:

Input ▼

```
SELECT cust_id
FROM orders
WHERE order_num IN (SELECT order_num
                    FROM orderitems
                    WHERE prod_id = 'TNT2');
```

Output ▼

```
+---------+
| cust_id |
+---------+
|   10001 |
|   10004 |
+---------+
```

Analysis ▼

Subqueries are always processed starting with the innermost SELECT statement and working outward. When the preceding SELECT statement is processed, Oracle actually performs two operations.

First, it runs the subquery:

```
SELECT order_num FROM orderitems WHERE prod_id='TNT2'
```

That query returns the two order numbers 20005 and 20007. Those two values are then passed to the WHERE clause of the outer query in the comma-delimited format required by the IN operator. The outer query now becomes

```
SELECT cust_id FROM orders WHERE order_num IN (20005,20007)
```

As you can see, the output is correct and exactly the same as the output returned by the previous hard-coded WHERE clause.

> TIP: **Formatting Your SQL**
>
> SELECT statements containing subqueries can be difficult to read and debug, especially as they grow in complexity. Breaking up the queries over multiple lines and indenting the lines appropriately as shown here can greatly simplify working with subqueries.

You now have the IDs of all the customers who ordered item TNT2. The next step is to retrieve the customer information for each of those customer IDs. The SQL statement to retrieve the two columns is as follows:

Input ▼

```
SELECT cust_name, cust_contact
FROM customers
WHERE cust_id IN (10001,10004);
```

Instead of hard-coding those customer IDs, you can turn this WHERE clause into yet another subquery:

Input ▼

```
SELECT cust_name, cust_contact
FROM customers
WHERE cust_id IN (SELECT cust_id
                  FROM orders
                  WHERE order_num IN (SELECT order_num
                                      FROM orderitems
                                      WHERE prod_id = 'TNT2'));
```

Output ▼

```
+----------------+---------------+
| cust_name      | cust_contact  |
+----------------+---------------+
| Coyote Inc.    | Y Lee         |
| Yosemite Place | Y Sam         |
+----------------+---------------+
```

Analysis ▼

To execute this `SELECT` statement, Oracle had to actually perform three `SELECT` statements. The innermost subquery returned a list of order numbers that were then used as the `WHERE` clause for the subquery above it. That subquery returned a list of customer IDs that were used as the `WHERE` clause for the top-level query. The top-level query actually returned the desired data.

As you can see, using subqueries in a `WHERE` clause enables you to write extremely powerful and flexible SQL statements. We nested three levels deep here, but if needed, you can nest far deeper than that. Just keep in mind that performance will start to deteriorate the further you nest queries.

> CAUTION: **Columns Must Match**
>
> When using a subquery in a `WHERE` clause (as shown here), make sure that the `SELECT` statement has the same number of columns as in the `WHERE` clause. Usually, a single column will be returned by the subquery and matched against a single column, but multiple columns may be used if needed.

Although usually used with the `IN` operator, subqueries can also be used to test for equality (using `=`), non-equality (using `<>`), and so on.

> NOTE: **Maximum Number of Subqueries**
>
> Oracle allows you to nest a maximum of 255 levels of subqueries within a `WHERE` clause (although you would be hard pressed to find a situation that warrants doing this!).

> CAUTION: **Subqueries and Performance**
>
> The code shown here works, and it achieves the desired result. However, using subqueries is not always the most efficient way to perform this type of data retrieval, although it might be. More on this is in Lesson 15, "Joining Tables," where you will revisit this same example.

Using Subqueries as Calculated Fields

Another way to use subqueries is in creating calculated fields. Suppose you want to display the total number of orders placed by every customer in your `customers` table. Orders are stored in the `orders` table along with the appropriate customer ID.

To perform this operation, follow these steps:

1. Retrieve the list of customers from the `customers` table.
2. For each customer retrieved, count the number of associated orders in the `orders` table.

As you learned in the previous two lessons, you can use `SELECT COUNT(*)` to count rows in a table, and by providing a `WHERE` clause to filter a specific customer ID, you can count just that customer's orders. For example, the following code counts the number of orders placed by customer `10001`:

Input ▼

```
SELECT COUNT(*) AS orders
FROM orders
WHERE cust_id = 10001;
```

To perform that `COUNT(*)` calculation for each customer, use `COUNT*` as a subquery. Look at the following code:

Input ▼

```
SELECT cust_name,
       cust_state,
       (SELECT COUNT(*)
        FROM orders
        WHERE orders.cust_id = customers.cust_id) AS orders
FROM customers
ORDER BY cust_name;
```

Output ▼

```
+---------------+------------+--------+
| cust_name     | cust_state | orders |
+---------------+------------+--------+
| Coyote Inc.   | MI         |      2 |
| E Fudd        | IL         |      1 |
| Mouse House   | OH         |      0 |
| Wascals       | IN         |      1 |
| Yosemite Place | AZ        |      1 |
+---------------+------------+--------+
```

Analysis ▼

This SELECT statement returns three columns for every customer in the customers table: cust_name, cust_state, and orders. orders is a calculated field that is set by a subquery provided in parentheses. That subquery is executed once for every customer retrieved. In this example, the subquery is executed five times because five customers were retrieved.

The WHERE clause in the subquery is a little different from the WHERE clauses used previously because it uses fully qualified column names (first mentioned in Lesson 4, "Retrieving Data"). The following clause tells SQL to compare the cust_id in the orders table to the one currently being retrieved from the customers table:

```
WHERE orders.cust_id = customers.cust_id
```

> **Correlated Subquery** A subquery that refers to the outer query.

The type of subquery is called a *correlated subquery*. This syntax—the table name and the column name separated by a period—must be used whenever there is possible ambiguity about column names. Why? Well, let's look at what happens if fully qualified column names are not used:

Input ▼

```
SELECT cust_name,
       cust_state,
       (SELECT COUNT(*)
        FROM orders
        WHERE cust_id = cust_id) AS orders
FROM customers
ORDER BY cust_name;
```

Output ▼

```
+----------------+------------+--------+
| cust_name      | cust_state | orders |
+----------------+------------+--------+
| Coyote Inc.    | MI         |      5 |
| E Fudd         | IL         |      5 |
| Mouse House    | OH         |      5 |
| Wascals        | IN         |      5 |
| Yosemite Place | AZ         |      5 |
+----------------+------------+--------+
```

Analysis ▼

Obviously the returned results are incorrect (compare them to the previous results), but why did this happen? There are two `cust_id` columns, one in `customers` and one in `orders`, and those two columns need to be compared to correctly match orders with their appropriate customers. Without fully qualifying the column names, Oracle assumes you are comparing the `cust_id` in the `orders` table to itself. And

```
SELECT COUNT(*) FROM orders WHERE cust_id = cust_id;
```

always returns the total number of orders in the `orders` table (because Oracle checks to see that every order's `cust_id` matches itself, which it always does, of course).

Although subqueries are extremely useful in constructing this type of `SELECT` statement, care must be taken to properly qualify ambiguous column names.

> NOTE: **Always More Than One Solution**
>
> As explained earlier in this lesson, although the sample code shown here works, it is often not the most efficient way to perform this type of data retrieval. You will revisit this example in a later lesson.

> TIP: **Build Queries with Subqueries Incrementally**
>
> Testing and debugging queries with subqueries can be tricky, particularly as these statements grow in complexity. The safest way to build (and test) queries with subqueries is to do so incrementally, in much the same way as Oracle processes them. Build and test the innermost query first. Then build and test the outer query with hard-coded data, and only after you have verified that it is working embed the subquery. Then test it again, and keep repeating these steps for each additional query. This will take just a little longer to construct your queries, but it saves you lots of time later (when you try to figure out why queries are not working) and significantly increases the likelihood of them working the first time.

> NOTE: `FROM` **Clause Subqueries**
>
> In addition to the subqueries used in `SELECT` and `WHERE` clauses shown in this lesson, Oracle also supports the use of subqueries in the `FROM` clause. This type of subquery is called an *inline view*, and it is a way to create a virtual table of sorts. Inline views are infrequently used and are thus not covered in this book, but views themselves are introduced in Lesson 21, "Using Views."

Summary

In this lesson, you learned what subqueries are and how to use them. The most common uses for subqueries are in `WHERE` clauses, in `IN` operators, and for populating calculated columns. You saw examples of both of these types of operations.

LESSON 15

Joining Tables

In this lesson, you'll learn what joins are, why they are used, and how to create SELECT *statements using them.*

Understanding Joins

One of SQL's most powerful features is the capability to join tables on the fly within data retrieval queries. Joins are one of the most important operations you can perform using SQL SELECT, and a good understanding of joins and join syntax is an extremely important part of learning SQL.

Before you can effectively use joins, you must understand relational tables and the basics of relational database design. What follows is by no means a complete coverage of the subject, but it should be enough to get you up and running.

Understanding Relational Tables

The best way to understand relational tables is to look at a real-world example.

Suppose you had a database table containing a product catalog, with each catalog item in its own row. The kind of information you would store with each item would include a product description and price, along with vendor information about the company that creates the product.

Now suppose you had multiple catalog items created by the same vendor. Where would you store the vendor information (things such as vendor name, address, and contact information)? You wouldn't want to store that data along with the products for several reasons:

- Because the vendor information is the same for each product that vendor produces, repeating the information for each product is a waste of time and storage space.

- If vendor information changes (for example, if the vendor moves or his area code changes), you would need to update every occurrence of the vendor information.
- When data is repeated (that is, the vendor information is used with each product), there is a high likelihood that the data will not be entered exactly the same way each time. Inconsistent data is extremely difficult to use in reporting.

The key here is that having multiple occurrences of the same data is never a good thing, and that principle is the basis for relational database design. Relational tables are designed so information is split into multiple tables, one for each data type. The tables are related to each other through common values (and thus the *relational* in relational design).

In our example, you can create two tables, one for vendor information and one for product information. The `vendors` table contains all the vendor information, one table row per vendor, along with a unique identifier for each vendor. This value, called a *primary key*, can be a vendor ID, or any other unique value. (Primary keys were first mentioned in Lesson 1, "Understanding SQL.")

The `products` table stores only product information, and no vendor-specific information other than the vendor ID (the `vendors` table's primary key). This key, called a *foreign key*, relates the `vendors` table to the `products` table, and using this vendor ID enables you to use the `vendors` table to find the details about the appropriate vendor.

> **Foreign Key** A column in one table that contains the primary key values from another table, thus defining the relationships between tables.

What does this do for you? Well, consider the following:

- Vendor information is never repeated, and so time and space are not wasted.
- If vendor information changes, you can update a single record in the `vendors` table. Data in related tables does not change.
- As no data is repeated, the data used is obviously consistent, making data reporting and manipulation much simpler.

The bottom line is that relational data can be stored efficiently and manipulated easily. Because of this, relational databases scale far better than non-relational databases.

> **Scale** Able to handle an increasing load without failing. A well-designed database or application is said to *scale well*.

Why Use Joins?

As just explained, breaking data into multiple tables enables more efficient storage, easier manipulation, and greater scalability. However, these benefits come with a price.

If data is stored in multiple tables, how can you retrieve that data with a single `SELECT` statement?

The answer is to use a join. Simply put, a *join* is a mechanism used to associate tables within a `SELECT` statement (and thus the name *join*). Using a special syntax, multiple tables can be joined so a single set of output is returned, and the join associates the correct rows in each table on-the-fly.

> NOTE: **Maintaining Referential Integrity**
>
> It is important to understand that a join is not a physical entity—in other words, it does not exist in the actual database tables. A join is created by Oracle as needed, and it persists for the duration of the query execution.
>
> When using relational tables, it is important that only valid data is inserted into relational columns. Going back to the example, if products were stored in the `products` table with an invalid vendor ID (one not present in the `vendors` table), those products would be inaccessible because they would not be related to any vendor.
>
> To prevent this from occurring, Oracle can be instructed to only allow valid values (ones present in the `vendors` table) in the vendor ID column in the `products` table. This is known as maintaining *referential integrity*, and is achieved by specifying the primary and foreign keys as part of the table definitions (as will be explained in Lesson 20, "Creating and Manipulating Tables").
>
> For an example of this, see the `create.sql` script used to create the `crashcourse` database tables. The `ALTER TABLE` statements at the end of the file are defining constrains to enforce referential integrity.

Creating a Join

Creating a join is very simple. You must specify all the tables to be included and how they are related to each other. Look at the following example:

Input ▼

```
SELECT vend_name, prod_name, prod_price
FROM vendors, products
WHERE vendors.vend_id = products.vend_id
ORDER BY vend_name, prod_name;
```

Output ▼

```
+-------------+----------------+------------+
| vend_name   | prod_name      | prod_price |
+-------------+----------------+------------+
| ACME        | Bird seed      |         10 |
| ACME        | Carrots        |        2.5 |
| ACME        | Detonator      |         13 |
| ACME        | Safe           |         50 |
| ACME        | Sling          |       4.49 |
| ACME        | TNT (1 stick)  |        2.5 |
| ACME        | TNT (5 sticks) |         10 |
| Anvils R Us | .5 ton anvil   |       5.99 |
| Anvils R Us | 1 ton anvil    |       9.99 |
| Anvils R Us | 2 ton anvil    |      14.99 |
| Jet Set     | JetPack 1000   |         35 |
| Jet Set     | JetPack 2000   |         55 |
| LT Supplies | Fuses          |       3.42 |
| LT Supplies | Oil can        |       8.99 |
+-------------+----------------+------------+
```

Analysis ▼

Take a look at the preceding code. The `SELECT` statement starts in the same way as all the statements you've looked at thus far, by specifying the columns to be retrieved. The big difference here is that two of the specified columns (`prod_name` and `prod_price`) are in one table, whereas the other (`vend_name`) is in another table.

Now look at the `FROM` clause. Unlike all the prior `SELECT` statements, this one has two tables listed in the `FROM` clause, `vendors` and `products`. These are the names of the two tables that are being joined in this `SELECT` statement. The tables are correctly joined with a `WHERE` clause that instructs Oracle to match `vend_id` in the `vendors` table with `vend_id` in the `products` table.

You'll notice that the columns are specified as `vendors.vend_id` and `products.vend_id`. This fully qualified column name is required here because if you just specified `vend_id`, Oracle cannot tell which `vend_id` columns you are referring to (as there are two of them, one in each table).

> CAUTION: **Fully Qualifying Column Names**
>
> You must use the fully qualified column name (table and column separated by a period) whenever there is a possible ambiguity about to which column you are referring. Oracle returns an error message if you refer to an ambiguous column name without fully qualifying it with a table name.

The Importance of the `WHERE` Clause

It might seem strange to use a `WHERE` clause to set the join relationship, but actually, there is a very good reason for this. Remember, when tables are joined in a `SELECT` statement, that relationship is constructed on the fly. Nothing in the database table definitions can instruct Oracle how to join the tables. You have to do that yourself. When you join two tables, what you are actually doing is pairing every row in the first table with every row in the second table. The `WHERE` clause acts as a filter to only include rows that match the specified filter condition—the join condition, in this case. Without the `WHERE` clause, every row in the first table is paired with every row in the second table, regardless of whether they logically go together.

> **Cartesian Product** The results returned by a table relationship without a join condition. The number of rows retrieved is the number of rows in the first table multiplied by the number of rows in the second table.

To understand this, look at the following `SELECT` statement and output:

Input ▼

```
SELECT vend_name, prod_name, prod_price
FROM vendors, products
ORDER BY vend_name, prod_name;
```

Output ▼

```
+-----------------+----------------+------------+
| vend_name       | prod_name      | prod_price |
+-----------------+----------------+------------+
| ACME            | .5 ton anvil   |       5.99 |
| ACME            | 1 ton anvil    |       9.99 |
| ACME            | 2 ton anvil    |      14.99 |
| ACME            | Bird seed      |         10 |
| ACME            | Carrots        |        2.5 |
| ACME            | Detonator      |         13 |
| ACME            | Fuses          |       3.42 |
| ACME            | JetPack 1000   |         35 |
| ACME            | JetPack 2000   |         55 |
| ACME            | Oil can        |       8.99 |
| ACME            | Safe           |         50 |
| ACME            | Sling          |       4.49 |
| ACME            | TNT (1 stick)  |        2.5 |
| ACME            | TNT (5 sticks) |         10 |
| Anvils R Us     | .5 ton anvil   |       5.99 |
| Anvils R Us     | 1 ton anvil    |       9.99 |
| Anvils R Us     | 2 ton anvil    |      14.99 |
| Anvils R Us     | Bird seed      |         10 |
| Anvils R Us     | Carrots        |        2.5 |
| Anvils R Us     | Detonator      |         13 |
| Anvils R Us     | Fuses          |       3.42 |
| Anvils R Us     | JetPack 1000   |         35 |
| Anvils R Us     | JetPack 2000   |         55 |
| Anvils R Us     | Oil can        |       8.99 |
| Anvils R Us     | Safe           |         50 |
| Anvils R Us     | Sling          |       4.49 |
| Anvils R Us     | TNT (1 stick)  |        2.5 |
| Anvils R Us     | TNT (5 sticks) |         10 |
| Furball Inc.    | .5 ton anvil   |       5.99 |
| Furball Inc.    | 1 ton anvil    |       9.99 |
| Furball Inc.    | 2 ton anvil    |      14.99 |
| Furball Inc.    | Bird seed      |         10 |
| Furball Inc.    | Carrots        |        2.5 |
| Furball Inc.    | Detonator      |         13 |
| Furball Inc.    | Fuses          |       3.42 |
| Furball Inc.    | JetPack 1000   |         35 |
```

```
| Furball Inc.     | JetPack 2000     |         55 |
| Furball Inc.     | Oil can          |       8.99 |
| Furball Inc.     | Safe             |         50 |
| Furball Inc.     | Sling            |       4.49 |
| Furball Inc.     | TNT (1 stick)    |        2.5 |
| Furball Inc.     | TNT (5 sticks)   |         10 |
| Jet Set          | .5 ton anvil     |       5.99 |
| Jet Set          | 1 ton anvil      |       9.99 |
| Jet Set          | 2 ton anvil      |      14.99 |
| Jet Set          | Bird seed        |         10 |
| Jet Set          | Carrots          |        2.5 |
| Jet Set          | Detonator        |         13 |
| Jet Set          | Fuses            |       3.42 |
| Jet Set          | JetPack 1000     |         35 |
| Jet Set          | JetPack 2000     |         55 |
| Jet Set          | Oil can          |       8.99 |
| Jet Set          | Safe             |         50 |
| Jet Set          | Sling            |       4.49 |
| Jet Set          | TNT (1 stick)    |        2.5 |
| Jet Set          | TNT (5 sticks)   |         10 |
| Jouets Et Ours   | .5 ton anvil     |       5.99 |
| Jouets Et Ours   | 1 ton anvil      |       9.99 |
| Jouets Et Ours   | 2 ton anvil      |      14.99 |
| Jouets Et Ours   | Bird seed        |         10 |
| Jouets Et Ours   | Carrots          |        2.5 |
| Jouets Et Ours   | Detonator        |         13 |
| Jouets Et Ours   | Fuses            |       3.42 |
| Jouets Et Ours   | JetPack 1000     |         35 |
| Jouets Et Ours   | JetPack 2000     |         55 |
| Jouets Et Ours   | Oil can          |       8.99 |
| Jouets Et Ours   | Safe             |         50 |
| Jouets Et Ours   | Sling            |       4.49 |
| Jouets Et Ours   | TNT (1 stick)    |        2.5 |
| Jouets Et Ours   | TNT (5 sticks)   |         10 |
| LT Supplies      | .5 ton anvil     |       5.99 |
| LT Supplies      | 1 ton anvil      |       9.99 |
| LT Supplies      | 2 ton anvil      |      14.99 |
| LT Supplies      | Bird seed        |         10 |
| LT Supplies      | Carrots          |        2.5 |
| LT Supplies      | Detonator        |         13 |
| LT Supplies      | Fuses            |       3.42 |
| LT Supplies      | JetPack 1000     |         35 |
| LT Supplies      | JetPack 2000     |         55 |
| LT Supplies      | Oil can          |       8.99 |
| LT Supplies      | Safe             |         50 |
| LT Supplies      | Sling            |       4.49 |
| LT Supplies      | TNT (1 stick)    |        2.5 |
| LT Supplies      | TNT (5 sticks)   |         10 |
+------------------+------------------+------------+
```

Analysis ▼

As you can see in the preceding output, the Cartesian product is seldom what you want. The data returned here has matched every product with every vendor, including products with the incorrect vendor (and even vendors with no products at all).

> CAUTION: **Don't Forget the `WHERE` Clause**
>
> Make sure all your joins have `WHERE` clauses, or Oracle returns far more data than you want. Similarly, make sure your `WHERE` clauses are correct. An incorrect filter condition causes Oracle to return incorrect data.

> TIP: **Cross Joins**
>
> Sometimes you'll hear the type of join that returns a Cartesian product referred to as a *cross join*.

Using Inner Joins

The join you have been using so far is called an *equijoin*—a join based on the testing of equality between two tables. This kind of join is also called an *inner join*. In fact, you may use a slightly different syntax for these joins, specifying the type of join explicitly. The following `SELECT` statement returns the exact same data as the preceding example:

Input ▼

```
SELECT vend_name, prod_name, prod_price
FROM vendors INNER JOIN products
 ON vendors.vend_id = products.vend_id;
```

Analysis ▼

The `SELECT` in the statement is the same as the preceding `SELECT` statement, but the `FROM` clause is different. Here the relationship between the two tables is part of the `FROM` clause specified as `INNER JOIN`. When using this syntax, the join condition is specified using the special `ON` clause instead of a `WHERE` clause. The actual condition passed to `ON` is the same as would be passed to `WHERE`.

> NOTE: **Which Syntax to Use?**
>
> Per the ANSI SQL specification, use of the `INNER JOIN` syntax is preferable. Furthermore, although using the `WHERE` clause to define joins is indeed simpler, using explicit join syntax ensures that you will never forget the join condition, and can impact performance, too (in some cases).
>
> Some SQL purists will insist that you use the `FROM` clause to define your joins. But I'm a huge fan of simplifying things, and Oracle (like every other DBMS vendor) has implemented support for the simpler syntax, so I use it extensively.
>
> Regardless, you're likely to run across both join syntaxes in the real world. As such, it's worthwhile to be familiar with the simplified `WHERE` clause joins and the ANSI preferred `FROM` clause joins.

Joining Multiple Tables

SQL imposes no limit to the number of tables that may be joined in a `SELECT` statement. The basic rules for creating the join remain the same. First list all the tables, and then define the relationship between each. Here is an example:

Input ▼

```
SELECT prod_name, vend_name, prod_price, quantity
FROM orderitems, products, vendors
WHERE products.vend_id = vendors.vend_id
  AND orderitems.prod_id = products.prod_id
  AND order_num = 20005;
```

Output ▼

```
+-----------------+-------------+------------+----------+
| prod_name       | vend_name   | prod_price | quantity |
+-----------------+-------------+------------+----------+
| .5 ton anvil    | Anvils R Us |       5.99 |       10 |
| 1 ton anvil     | Anvils R Us |       9.99 |        3 |
| TNT (5 sticks)  | ACME        |         10 |        5 |
| Bird seed       | ACME        |         10 |        1 |
+-----------------+-------------+------------+----------+
```

Analysis ▼

This example displays the items in order number `20005`. Order items are stored in the `orderitems` table. Each product is stored by its product ID, which refers to a product in the `products` table. The products are linked to the appropriate vendor in the `vendors` table by the vendor ID, which is stored with each product record. The `FROM` clause here lists the three tables, and the `WHERE` clause defines both of those join conditions. An additional `WHERE` condition is then used to filter just the items for order `20005`.

> CAUTION: **Performance Considerations**
>
> Oracle processes joins at runtime, relating each table as specified. This process can become very resource intensive, so be careful not to join tables unnecessarily. The more tables you join, the more performance degrades.

Now would be a good time to revisit the following example from Lesson 14, "Working with Subqueries." As you will recall, this `SELECT` statement returns a list of customers who ordered product `TNT2`:

Input ▼

```
SELECT cust_name, cust_contact
FROM customers
WHERE cust_id IN (SELECT cust_id
                  FROM orders
                  WHERE order_num IN (SELECT order_num
                                      FROM orderitems
                                      WHERE prod_id = 'TNT2'));
```

As mentioned in Lesson 14, subqueries might not always the most efficient way to perform complex `SELECT` operations, and so as promised, here is the same query using joins:

Input ▼

```
SELECT cust_name, cust_contact
FROM customers, orders, orderitems
WHERE customers.cust_id = orders.cust_id
  AND orderitems.order_num = orders.order_num
  AND prod_id = 'TNT2';
```

Output ▼

```
+----------------+--------------+
| cust_name      | cust_contact |
+----------------+--------------+
| Coyote Inc.    | Y Lee        |
| Yosemite Place | Y Sam        |
+----------------+--------------+
```

Analysis ▼

As explained in Lesson 14, returning the data needed in this query requires the use of three tables. But instead of using them within nested subqueries, here two joins are used to connect the tables. There are three WHERE clause conditions here. The first two connect the tables in the join, and the last one filters the data for product TNT2.

Here is the same statement, this time with the join implemented in the FROM clause:

Input ▼

```
SELECT cust_name, cust_contact
FROM customers
INNER JOIN orders ON customers.cust_id = orders.cust_id
INNER JOIN orderitems ON orderitems.order_num = orders.order_num
WHERE prod_id = 'TNT2';
```

Analysis ▼

Once again, three tables are joined. FROM specifies the first table, and then two INNER JOIN statements join the additional tables, with an ON clause defining their relationship. The output would be exactly the same as in the preceding example.

> TIP: **It Pays to Experiment**
>
> As you can see, there is often more than one way to perform any given SQL operation, and there is rarely a definitive right or wrong way. Performance can be affected by the type of operation, the amount of data in the tables, whether indexes and keys are

present, and a whole slew of other criteria. Therefore, it is often worth experimenting with different selection mechanisms to find the one that works best for you.

Summary

Joins are one of the most important and powerful features in SQL, and using them effectively requires a basic understanding of relational database design. In this lesson, you learned some of the basics of relational database design as an introduction to learning about joins. You also learned how to create an equijoin (also known as an inner join), which is the most commonly used form of join. In the next lesson, you'll learn how to create other types of joins.

LESSON 16

Creating Advanced Joins

In this lesson, you'll learn all about additional join types—what they are and how to use them. You'll also learn how to use table aliases and how to use aggregate functions with joined tables.

Using Table Aliases

Back in Lesson 10, "Creating Calculated Fields," you learned how to use aliases to refer to retrieved table columns. The syntax to alias a column looks like this:

Input ▼

```
SELECT RTrim(vend_name) || ', (' || RTrim(vend_country) || ')'
➥AS vend_title
FROM vendors
ORDER BY vend_name;
```

In addition to using aliases for column names and calculated fields, SQL also enables you to alias table names. There are two primary reasons to do this:

- To shorten the SQL syntax
- To enable multiple uses of the same table within a single SELECT statement

Take a look at the following SELECT statement. It is basically the same statement as an example used in the previous lesson, but it has been modified to use aliases:

Input ▼

```
SELECT cust_name, cust_contact
FROM customers c, orders o, orderitems oi
WHERE c.cust_id = o.cust_id
  AND oi.order_num = o.order_num
  AND prod_id = 'TNT2';
```

Analysis ▼

Notice that the three tables in the `FROM` clauses all have aliases. `customers c` establishes `c` as an alias for `customers`, and so on. This enables you to use the abbreviated `c` instead of the full text `customers`. In this example, the table aliases were used only in the `WHERE` clause, but aliases are not limited to just `WHERE`. You can use aliases in the `SELECT` list, the `ORDER BY` clause, and in any other part of the statement as well.

> NOTE: **No** `AS`
>
> Unlike most other DBMSs, Oracle does not use the `AS` keyword for table aliases; thus, `customers c` is correct, but `customers AS c` would throw an error.

It is also worth noting that table aliases are only used during query execution. Unlike column aliases, table aliases are never returned to the client.

Using Different Join Types

So far, you have used only simple joins known as inner joins or *equijoins*. You'll now take a look at three additional join types: the self join, the natural join, and the outer join.

Self Joins

As mentioned earlier, one of the primary reasons to use table aliases is to be able to refer to the same table more than once in a single `SELECT` statement. An example will demonstrate this.

Suppose that a problem was found with a product (item id DTNTR), and you therefore wanted to know all the products made by the same vendor to determine whether the problem applied to them, too. This query requires that you first find out which vendor creates item DTNTR, and next find which other products are made by the same vendor. The following is one way to approach this problem:

Input ▼

```
SELECT prod_id, prod_name
FROM products
WHERE vend_id = (SELECT vend_id
                 FROM products
                 WHERE prod_id = 'DTNTR');
```

Output ▼

```
+---------+-----------------+
| prod_id | prod_name       |
+---------+-----------------+
| DTNTR   | Detonator       |
| FB      | Bird seed       |
| FC      | Carrots         |
| SAFE    | Safe            |
| SLING   | Sling           |
| TNT1    | TNT (1 stick)   |
| TNT2    | TNT (5 sticks)  |
+---------+-----------------+
```

Analysis ▼

This first solution uses subqueries. The inner SELECT statement does a simple retrieval to return the vend_id of the vendor that makes item DTNTR. That ID is the one used in the WHERE clause of the outer query so all items produced by that vendor are retrieved. (You learned all about subqueries in Lesson 14, "Working with Subqueries." Refer to that lesson for more information.)

Now look at the same query using a join, and I'll present the code using both join formats:

Input ▼

```
SELECT p1.prod_id, p1.prod_name
FROM products p1, products p2
WHERE p1.vend_id = p2.vend_id
  AND p2.prod_id = 'DTNTR';
```

Input ▼

```
SELECT p1.prod_id, p1.prod_name
FROM products p1
INNER JOIN products p2 ON p1.vend_id = p2.vend_id
WHERE p2.prod_id = 'DTNTR';
```

Output ▼

```
+---------+----------------+
| prod_id | prod_name      |
+---------+----------------+
| DTNTR   | Detonator      |
| FB      | Bird seed      |
| FC      | Carrots        |
| SAFE    | Safe           |
| SLING   | Sling          |
| TNT1    | TNT (1 stick)  |
| TNT2    | TNT (5 sticks) |
+---------+----------------+
```

Analysis ▼

The two tables needed in this query are actually the same table, and so the `products` table appears twice. Although this is perfectly legal, any references to table `products` would be ambiguous because Oracle could not know to which instance of the `products` tables you are referring.

To resolve this problem, table aliases are used. The first occurrence of `products` has an alias of `p1`, and the second has an alias of `p2`. Now those aliases can be used as table names. The `SELECT` statement, for example, uses the `p1` prefix to explicitly state the full name of the desired columns. If it did not, Oracle would return an error because there are two columns named `prod_id` and `prod_name`. It cannot know which one you want (even though, in truth, they are one and the same). The `WHERE` or `ON` clauses join the tables (by matching `vend_id` in `p1` to `vend_id` in `p2`), and results are filtered by `prod_id` in the second table to return only the desired data.

> TIP: **Self Joins Instead of Subqueries**
>
> Self joins are often used to replace statements using subqueries that retrieve data from the same table as the outer statement. Although the end result is the same, sometimes these joins execute far more quickly than they do subqueries. It is usually worth experimenting with both to determine which performs better.

Natural Joins

Whenever tables are joined, at least one column appears in more than one table (the columns being joined). Standard joins (the inner joins you learned about in the previous lesson) return all data, even multiple occurrences of the same column. A *natural join* simply eliminates those multiple occurrences so only one of each column is returned.

How does it do this? The answer is it doesn't—you do it. A natural join is a join in which you select only columns that are unique. This is typically done using a wildcard (`SELECT *`) for one table and explicit subsets of the columns for all other tables. The following is an example, once again, presented using both join syntaxes:

Input ▼

```
SELECT c.*, o.order_num, o.order_date,
       oi.prod_id, oi.quantity, OI.item_price
FROM customers c, orders o, orderitems oi
WHERE c.cust_id = o.cust_id
  AND oi.order_num = o.order_num
  AND prod_id = 'FB';
```

Input ▼

```
SELECT c.*, o.order_num, o.order_date,
       oi.prod_id, oi.quantity, OI.item_price
FROM customers c
INNER JOIN orders o ON c.cust_id = o.cust_id
INNER JOIN orderitems oi ON oi.order_num = o.order_num
WHERE prod_id = 'FB';
```

Analysis ▼

In these examples, a wildcard is used for the first table only, and so all columns from `c` (the `customers` table) are returned. All other columns are explicitly listed so no duplicate columns are retrieved.

The truth is, every inner join you have created thus far is actually a natural join, and you will probably never even need an inner join that is not a natural join.

Outer Joins

Most joins relate rows in one table with rows in another. But occasionally, you want to include rows that have no related rows. For example, you might use joins to accomplish the following tasks:

- Count how many orders each customer placed, including customers who have yet to place an order
- List all products with order quantities, including products not ordered by anyone
- Calculate average sale sizes, taking into account customers who have not yet placed an order

In each of these examples, the join includes table rows that have no associated rows in the related table. This type of join is called an *outer join.*

The following `SELECT` statement is a simple inner join. It retrieves a list of all customers and their orders:

Input ▼

```
SELECT customers.cust_id, orders.order_num
FROM customers
INNER JOIN orders ON customers.cust_id = orders.cust_id;
```

Outer join syntax is similar. To retrieve a list of all customers, including those who have placed no orders, you can do the following:

Input ▼

```
SELECT customers.cust_id, orders.order_num
FROM customers
LEFT OUTER JOIN orders ON customers.cust_id = orders.cust_id;
```

Output ▼

```
+---------+-----------+
| cust_id | order_num |
+---------+-----------+
|   10001 |     20005 |
|   10001 |     20009 |
|   10002 |           |
|   10003 |     20006 |
|   10004 |     20007 |
|   10005 |     20008 |
+---------+-----------+
```

Analysis ▼

Like the inner join shown in the previous lesson, this SELECT statement uses the keywords OUTER JOIN to specify the join type (instead of specifying it in the WHERE clause). But unlike inner joins, which relate rows in both tables, outer joins also include rows with no related rows. When using OUTER JOIN syntax, you must use the RIGHT or LEFT keywords to specify the table from which to include all rows (RIGHT for the one on the right of OUTER JOIN, and LEFT for the one on the left). The previous example uses LEFT OUTER JOIN to select all the rows from the table on the left in the FROM clause (the customers table). To select all the rows from the table on the right, you use a RIGHT OUTER JOIN, as shown in this example:

Input ▼

```
SELECT customers.cust_id, orders.order_num
FROM customers
RIGHT OUTER JOIN orders ON orders.cust_id = customers.cust_id;
```

> NOTE: **No *= Or *=**
>
> Oracle does not support the use of the simplified *= and =* OUTER JOIN syntax popularized by other DBMSs.

> TIP: **Outer Join Types**
>
> There are two basic forms of outer joins—the left outer join and the right outer join. The only difference between them is the order of the tables they are relating. In other words, a left outer join can be turned into a right outer join simply by reversing the order of the tables in the `FROM` or `WHERE` clause. As such, the two types of outer join can be used interchangeably, and the decision about which one to use is based purely on convenience.

Using Joins with Aggregate Functions

As you learned in Lesson 12, "Summarizing Data," aggregate functions are used to summarize data. Although all the examples of aggregate functions thus far only summarized data from a single table, these functions can also be used with joins.

To demonstrate this, let's look at an example. You want to retrieve a list of all customers and the number of orders that each has placed. The following code uses the `COUNT()` function to achieve this:

Input ▼

```
SELECT customers.cust_name,
       COUNT(orders.order_num) AS num_ord
FROM customers
INNER JOIN orders ON customers.cust_id = orders.cust_id
GROUP BY customers.cust_name;
```

Output ▼

```
+----------------+---------+
| cust_name      | num_ord |
+----------------+---------+
| Coyote Inc.    |       2 |
| Wascals        |       1 |
| Yosemite Place |       1 |
| E Fudd         |       1 |
+----------------+---------+
```

Analysis ▼

This SELECT statement uses INNER JOIN to relate the customers and orders tables to each other. The GROUP BY clause groups the data by customer, and so the function call COUNT(orders.order_num) counts the number of orders for each customer and returns it as num_ord.

Aggregate functions can be used just as easily with other join types. See the following example:

Input ▼

```
SELECT customers.cust_name,
       COUNT(orders.order_num) AS num_ord
FROM customers
LEFT OUTER JOIN orders ON customers.cust_id = orders.cust_id
GROUP BY customers.cust_name;
```

Output ▼

```
+----------------+---------+
| cust_name      | num_ord |
+----------------+---------+
| Coyote Inc.    |       2 |
| Mouse House    |       0 |
| Wascals        |       1 |
| Yosemite Place |       1 |
| E Fudd         |       1 |
+----------------+---------+
```

Analysis ▼

This example uses a left outer join to include all customers, even those who have not placed any orders. The results show that customer Mouse House (with 0 orders) is also included this time.

Using Joins and Join Conditions

Before wrapping up this two-lesson discussion on joins, it is worthwhile to summarize some key points regarding joins and their use:

- Pay careful attention to the type of join being used. More often than not, you'll want an inner join, but there are often valid uses for outer joins, too.
- Make sure you use the correct join condition, or you'll return incorrect data.
- Make sure you always provide a join condition, or you'll end up with the Cartesian product.
- You may include multiple tables in a join and even have different join types for each. Although this is legal and often useful, make sure you test each join separately before testing them together. This makes troubleshooting far simpler.

Summary

This lesson was a continuation of the previous lesson on joins. This lesson started by teaching you how and why to use aliases, and then continued with a discussion on different join types and various forms of syntax used with each. You also learned how to use aggregate functions with joins, and some important do's and don'ts to keep in mind when working with joins.

LESSON 17
Combining Queries

In this lesson, you'll learn how to use the `UNION` *operator to combine multiple* `SELECT` *statements into one result set.*

Understanding Combined Queries

Most SQL queries contain a single `SELECT` statement that returns data from one or more tables. Oracle also enables you to perform multiple queries (multiple `SELECT` statements) and return the results as a single query result set. These combined queries are usually known as *unions* or *compound queries*.

There are basically two scenarios in which you would use combined queries:

- To return similarly structured data from different tables in a single query
- To perform multiple queries against a single table returning the data as one query

> TIP: **Combining Queries and Multiple** `WHERE` **Conditions**
>
> For the most part, combining two queries to the same table accomplishes the same thing as a single query with multiple `WHERE` clause conditions. In other words, any `SELECT` statement with multiple `WHERE` clauses can also be specified as a combined query, as you'll see in the section that follows. However, the performance of each of the two techniques can vary based on the queries used. As such, it is always good to experiment to determine which is preferable for specific queries.

Creating Combined Queries

SQL queries are combined using the UNION operator. Using UNION, multiple SELECT statements can be specified, and their results can be combined into a single result set.

Using UNION

Using UNION is simple enough. All you do is specify each SELECT statement and place the keyword UNION between each.

Let's look at an example. You need a list of all products costing 5 or less. You also want to include all products made by vendors 1001 and 1002, regardless of price. Of course, you can create a WHERE clause that will do this, but this time you'll use a UNION instead.

As just explained, creating a UNION involves writing multiple SELECT statements. First, look at the individual statements:

Input ▼

```
SELECT vend_id, prod_id, prod_price
FROM products
WHERE prod_price <= 5;
```

Output ▼

```
+---------+---------+------------+
| vend_id | prod_id | prod_price |
+---------+---------+------------+
|    1003 | FC      |        2.5 |
|    1002 | FU1     |       3.42 |
|    1003 | SLING   |       4.49 |
|    1003 | TNT1    |        2.5 |
+---------+---------+------------+
```

Input ▼

```
SELECT vend_id, prod_id, prod_price
FROM products
WHERE vend_id IN (1001,1002);
```

Output ▼

```
+---------+---------+------------+
| vend_id | prod_id | prod_price |
+---------+---------+------------+
|    1001 | ANV01   |       5.99 |
|    1001 | ANV02   |       9.99 |
|    1001 | ANV03   |      14.99 |
|    1002 | FU1     |       3.42 |
|    1002 | OL1     |       8.99 |
+---------+---------+------------+
```

Analysis ▼

The first `SELECT` retrieves all products with a price of no more than `5`. The second `SELECT` uses `IN` to find all products made by vendors `1001` and `1002`.

To combine these two statements, do the following:

Input ▼

```
SELECT vend_id, prod_id, prod_price
FROM products
WHERE prod_price <= 5
UNION
SELECT vend_id, prod_id, prod_price
FROM products
WHERE vend_id IN (1001,1002);
```

Output ▼

```
+---------+---------+------------+
| vend_id | prod_id | prod_price |
+---------+---------+------------+
|    1003 | FC      |        2.5 |
|    1002 | FU1     |       3.42 |
|    1003 | SLING   |       4.49 |
|    1003 | TNT1    |        2.5 |
|    1001 | ANV01   |       5.99 |
|    1001 | ANV02   |       9.99 |
|    1001 | ANV03   |      14.99 |
|    1002 | OL1     |       8.99 |
+---------+---------+------------+
```

Analysis ▼

The preceding statements are made up of both of the previous SELECT statements separated by the UNION keyword. UNION instructs Oracle to execute both SELECT statements and combine the output into a single query result set.

As a point of reference, here is the same query using multiple WHERE clauses instead of a UNION:

Input ▼

```
SELECT vend_id, prod_id, prod_price
FROM products
WHERE prod_price <= 5
  OR vend_id IN (1001,1002);
```

In this simple example, the UNION might actually be more complicated than using a WHERE clause. But with more complex filtering conditions, or if the data is being retrieved from multiple tables (and not just a single table), the UNION could have made the process much simpler.

UNION Rules

As you can see, unions are very easy to use, but a few rules govern exactly which queries can be combined:

- A UNION must be comprised of two or more SELECT statements, each separated by the keyword UNION (so, if combining four SELECT statements, three UNION keywords would be used).
- Each query in a UNION must contain the same columns, expressions, or aggregate functions (although columns need not be listed in the same order).
- Column datatypes must be compatible. They need not be the exact same type, but they must be of a type that Oracle can implicitly convert (for example, different numeric types or different date types).

Aside from these basic rules and restrictions, unions can be used for any data retrieval tasks.

Including or Eliminating Duplicate Rows

Go back to the preceding section titled "Using UNION" and look at the sample SELECT statements used. You'll notice that when executed individually, the first SELECT statement returns four rows, and the second SELECT statement returns five rows. However, when the two SELECT statements are combined with a UNION, only eight rows are returned, not nine.

The UNION automatically removes any duplicate rows from the query result set (in other words, it behaves just as multiple WHERE clause conditions in a single SELECT would). Because vendor 1002 creates a product that costs less than 5, that row was returned by both SELECT statements. When the UNION was used, the duplicate row was eliminated.

This is the default behavior of UNION, but you can change this if you so desire. If you do, in fact, want all occurrences of all matches returned, you can use UNION ALL instead of UNION.

Look at the following example:

Input ▼

```
SELECT vend_id, prod_id, prod_price
FROM products
WHERE prod_price <= 5
UNION ALL
SELECT vend_id, prod_id, prod_price
FROM products
WHERE vend_id IN (1001,1002);
```

Output ▼

```
+---------+---------+------------+
| vend_id | prod_id | prod_price |
+---------+---------+------------+
|    1003 | FC      |        2.5 |
|    1002 | FU1     |       3.42 |
|    1003 | SLING   |       4.49 |
|    1003 | TNT1    |        2.5 |
|    1001 | ANV01   |       5.99 |
|    1001 | ANV02   |       9.99 |
|    1001 | ANV03   |      14.99 |
|    1002 | FU1     |       3.42 |
|    1002 | OL1     |       8.99 |
+---------+---------+------------+
```

Analysis ▼

Using UNION ALL, Oracle does not eliminate duplicates. Therefore, the preceding example returns nine rows, one of them occurring twice.

> TIP: UNION **versus** WHERE
>
> The beginning of this lesson said that UNION almost always accomplishes the same thing as multiple WHERE conditions. UNION ALL is the form of UNION that accomplishes what cannot be done with WHERE clauses. If you do, in fact, want all occurrences of matches for every condition (including duplicates), you must use UNION ALL and not WHERE.

Sorting Combined Query Results

SELECT statement output is sorted using the ORDER BY clause. When combining queries with a UNION, only one ORDER BY clause may be used, and it must occur after the final SELECT statement. There is very little point in sorting part of a result set one way and part another way, and so multiple ORDER BY clauses are not allowed.

The following example sorts the results returned by the previously used UNION:

Input ▼

```
SELECT vend_id, prod_id, prod_price
FROM products
WHERE prod_price <= 5
UNION
SELECT vend_id, prod_id, prod_price
FROM products
WHERE vend_id IN (1001,1002)
ORDER BY vend_id, prod_price;
```

Output ▼

```
+---------+---------+------------+
| vend_id | prod_id | prod_price |
+---------+---------+------------+
|    1001 | ANV01   |       5.99 |
|    1001 | ANV02   |       9.99 |
|    1001 | ANV03   |      14.99 |
|    1002 | FU1     |       3.42 |
|    1002 | OL1     |       8.99 |
|    1003 | TNT1    |        2.5 |
|    1003 | FC      |        2.5 |
|    1003 | SLING   |       4.49 |
+---------+---------+------------+
```

Analysis ▼

This UNION takes a single ORDER BY clause after the final SELECT statement. Even though the ORDER BY appears to only be a part of that last SELECT statement, Oracle will in fact use it to sort all the results returned by all the SELECT statements.

> NOTE: **Combining Different Tables**
>
> For the sake of simplicity, all the examples in this lesson combined queries using the same table. However, everything you learned here also applies to using UNION to combine queries of different tables.

Summary

In this lesson, you learned how to combine SELECT statements with the UNION operator. Using UNION, you can return the results of multiple queries as one combined query, either including or excluding duplicates. The use of UNION can greatly simplify complex WHERE clauses and retrieving data from multiple tables.

LESSON 18

Inserting Data

In this lesson, you will learn how to insert data into tables using the SQL `INSERT` statement.

Understanding Data Insertion

`SELECT` is undoubtedly the most frequently used SQL statement (which is why the past 15 lessons were dedicated to it). But there are three other frequently used SQL statements that you should learn. The first one is `INSERT`. (You'll get to the other two, `UPDATE` and `DELETE`, in the next lesson.)

As its name suggests, `INSERT` is used to insert (add) rows to a database table. Insert can be used in several ways:

- To insert a single complete row
- To insert a single partial row
- To insert multiple rows
- To insert the results of a query

You'll now look at each of these.

> TIP: `INSERT` **and System Security**
>
> Use of the `INSERT` statement can be disabled per table or per user using Oracle security, as explained in Lesson 26, "Managing Security."

Inserting Complete Rows

The simplest way to insert data into a table is to use the basic `INSERT` syntax, which requires that you specify the table name and the values to be inserted into the new row. Here is an example of this:

Input ▼

```
INSERT INTO Customers
VALUES(10006,
       'Pep E. LaPew',
       '100 Main Street',
       'Los Angeles',
       'CA',
       '90046',
       'USA',
       NULL,
       NULL);
```

> NOTE: **No Output**
>
> `INSERT` statements usually generate no output, but if you execute the preceding statement in Oracle SQL Developer, you should see a `1 row inserted.` message.

Analysis ▼

The preceding example inserts a new customer into the `customers` table. The data to be stored in each table column is specified in the `VALUES` clause, and a value must be provided for every column. If a column has no value (for example, the `cust_contact` and `cust_email` columns), the `NULL` value should be used (assuming the table allows no value to be specified for that column). The columns must be populated in the order in which they appear in the table definition.

Although this syntax is indeed simple, it is not at all safe and should generally be avoided at all costs. The previous SQL statement is highly dependent on the order in which the columns are defined in the table. It also depends on information about that order being readily available. Even if it is available, there is no guarantee that the columns will be in the exact same order the next time the table is reconstructed. Therefore, writing

SQL statements that depend on specific column ordering is very unsafe. If you do so, something will inevitably break at some point.

The safer (and unfortunately more cumbersome) way to write the INSERT statement is as follows:

Input ▼

```
INSERT INTO customers(cust_id,
                      cust_name,
                      cust_address,
                      cust_city,
                      cust_state,
                      cust_zip,
                      cust_country
)
VALUES(10006,
       'Pep E. LaPew',
       '100 Main Street',
       'Los Angeles',
       'CA',
       '90046',
       'USA'
);
```

> NOTE: **Can't `INSERT` Twice**
>
> If you executed this latest INSERT statement, you would have seen an error message complaining `unique constraint violated`. This is because the `cust_id` field is a primary key and so every customer must have a unique `cust_id`. As both examples used the same `10006` value, Oracle can't accept the second insertion. You can simply address this problem by using `10007` as the `cust_id`, and if you are going to insert additional rows, keep incrementing that number.

Analysis ▼

This example does the exact same thing as the previous INSERT statement, but this time, the column names are explicitly stated in parentheses after the table name. When the row is inserted, Oracle matches each item in the columns list with the appropriate value in the VALUES list. The first entry in VALUES corresponds to the first specified column name. The second value corresponds to the second column name, and so on.

> NOTE: **Automatic Primary Keys**
>
> Some table columns need unique values; for example, order numbers, employee IDs, or (as in the example just shown) customer IDs. Rather than have to assign unique values manually each time a row is added (and having to keep track of what value was last used), most DBMSs provide a way to automatically assign the next available number for you each time a row is added to a table. This functionality is known as *auto increment*. Unfortunately, Oracle only added support for auto increment in version 12c; users of prior versions (including Oracle Express Edition) can't use auto increment and have to resort to other techniques to keep track of the next available identifier. As this book is intended to be used by Oracle 10g, 11g, and 12c users, I opted not to use Oracle's new auto increment functionality. However, if you are using Oracle 12c, feel free to take advantage of this long-awaited enhancement.

Because column names are provided, the VALUES must match the specified column names in the order in which they are specified, and not necessarily in the order that the columns appear in the actual table. The advantage of this is that, even if the table layout changes, the INSERT statement still works correctly. You'll also notice that the columns with NULL values (the final two) were not listed in the column list and so no values were needed.

The following INSERT statement populates all the row columns (just as before), but it does so in a different order. Because the column names are specified, the insertion works correctly:

Input ▼

```
INSERT INTO customers(cust_id,
            cust_name,
            cust_contact,
            cust_email,
            cust_address,
            cust_city,
            cust_state,
            cust_zip,
            cust_country)
```

```
VALUES(10006,
      'Pep E. LaPew',
      NULL,
      NULL,
      '100 Main Street',
      'Los Angeles',
      'CA',
      '90046',
      'USA');
```

> TIP: **Always Use a Column List**
>
> As a rule, never use `INSERT` without explicitly specifying the column list. This greatly increases the probability that your SQL will continue to function in the event that table changes occur.

> CAUTION: **Use `VALUES` Carefully**
>
> Regardless of the `INSERT` syntax being used, the correct number of `VALUES` must be specified. If no column names are provided, a value must be present for every table column. If column names are provided, a value must be present for each listed column. If none is present, an error message will be generated, and the row will not be inserted.

Using this syntax, you can also omit columns. This means you only provide values for some columns, but not for others. (You've actually already seen an example of this: `cust_id` was omitted when column names were explicitly listed.)

> CAUTION: **Omitting Columns**
>
> You may omit columns from an `INSERT` operation if the table definition so allows. One of the following conditions must exist:
>
> - The column is defined as allowing `NULL` values (no value at all).
> - A default value is specified in the table definition. This means the default value will be used if no value is specified.
>
> If you omit a value from a table that does not allow `NULL` values and does not have a default, Oracle generates an error message, and the row is not inserted.

> TIP: **Inserting Multiple Rows**
>
> Unlike most other DBMSs, Oracle doesn't support a version of `INSERT` that can insert multiple rows at once. There are workarounds (using the `dual` table I've mentioned previously), but in practice you'll probably just use multiple INSERT statements (as we did in the `populate.sql` file back in Lesson 3, "Working with Oracle").

Inserting Retrieved Data

`INSERT` is usually used to add a row to a table using specified values. There is another form of `INSERT` that can be used to insert the result of a `SELECT` statement into a table. This is known as `INSERT SELECT`, and, as its name suggests, it is made up of an `INSERT` statement and a `SELECT` statement.

Suppose you want to merge a list of customers from another table into your `customers` table. Instead of reading one row at a time and inserting it with `INSERT`, you can do the following:

> NOTE: **Instructions Needed for the Next Example**
>
> The following example imports data from a table named `custnew` into the `customers` table. To try this example, create a new table named `custnew` using the `CREATE TABLE customers` statement in `create.sql`, and obviously replacing `customers` with `custnew`. Then add a few customers of your own, being careful to not use `cust_id` values that were already used in `customers` (the subsequent `INSERT` operation will fail if primary key values are duplicated). The easiest way to do this is just start the numbers much higher, perhaps at `20000`.

Input ▼

```
INSERT INTO customers(cust_id,
                      cust_contact,
                      cust_email,
                      cust_name,
                      cust_address,
```

```
                    cust_city,
                    cust_state,
                    cust_zip,
                    cust_country)
SELECT cust_id,
       cust_contact,
       cust_email,
       cust_name,
       cust_address,
       cust_city,
       cust_state,
       cust_zip,
       cust_country
FROM custnew;
```

Analysis ▼

This example uses `INSERT SELECT` to import all the data from `custnew` into `customers`. Instead of listing the `VALUES` to be inserted, the `SELECT` statement retrieves them from `custnew`. Each column in the `SELECT` corresponds to a column in the specified columns list. How many rows will this statement insert? That depends on how many rows are in the `custnew` table. If the table is empty, no rows are inserted (and no error will be generated because the operation is still valid). If the table does, in fact, contain data, all that data is inserted into `customers`.

> TIP: **Column Names in** `INSERT SELECT`
>
> This example uses the same column names in both the `INSERT` and `SELECT` statements for simplicity's sake, but there is no requirement that the column names match. In fact, Oracle does not even pay attention to the column names returned by the `SELECT`. Rather, the column position is used, so the first column in the `SELECT` (regardless of its name) will be used to populate the first specified table column, and so on. This is very useful when importing data from tables that use different column names.

The `SELECT` statement used in an `INSERT SELECT` can include a `WHERE` clause to filter the data to be inserted.

> TIP: **More Examples**
>
> Looking for more examples of `INSERT` use? See the example table population scripts used back in Lesson 3 to populate the example tables used in this book.

Summary

In this lesson, you learned how to use `INSERT` to insert rows into a database table. You learned several other ways to use `INSERT`, and why explicit column specification is preferred. You also learned how to use `INSERT SELECT` to import rows from another table. In the next lesson, you'll learn how to use `UPDATE` and `DELETE` to further manipulate table data.

LESSON 19
Updating and Deleting Data

In this lesson, you will learn how to use the `UPDATE` and `DELETE` statements to enable you to further manipulate your table data.

Updating Data

To update (modify) data in a table, the `UPDATE` statement is used. `UPDATE` can be used in two ways:

- To update specific rows in a table
- To update all rows in a table

Let's take a look at each of these uses.

> CAUTION: **Don't Omit the `WHERE` Clause**
> Special care must be exercised when using `UPDATE` because it is all too easy to mistakenly update every row in your table. Please read this entire section on `UPDATE` before using this statement.

> TIP: **`UPDATE` and Security**
> Use of the `UPDATE` statement can be restricted and controlled. More on this in Lesson 26, "Managing Security."

The UPDATE statement is very easy to use—some would say too easy. The basic format of an UPDATE statement is made up of three parts:

- The table to be updated
- The column names and their new values
- The filter condition that determines which rows should be updated

Let's take a look at a simple example. Customer 10005 now has an email address, and so his record needs updating. The following statement performs this update:

Input ▼

```
UPDATE customers
SET cust_email = 'elmer@fudd.com'
WHERE cust_id = 10005;
```

The UPDATE statement always begins with the name of the table being updated. In this example, it is the customers table. The SET command is then used to assign the new value to a column. As used here, the SET clause sets the cust_email column to the specified value:

```
SET cust_email = 'elmer@fudd.com'
```

The UPDATE statement finishes with a WHERE clause that tells Oracle which row to update. Without a WHERE clause, Oracle would update all the rows in the customers table with this new email address—definitely not the desired effect.

> NOTE: **No Output**
>
> UPDATE statements usually generate no output, but if you execute the preceding statement in Oracle SQL Developer, you should see a `1 row updated.` message. If more than one row was updated, well, that probably means that you omitted (or mistyped) the WHERE clause.

Updating multiple columns requires a slightly different syntax:

Input ▼

```
UPDATE customers
SET cust_name = 'The Fudds',
    cust_email = 'elmer@fudd.com'
WHERE cust_id = 10005;
```

When updating multiple columns, only a single `SET` command is used, and each `column = value` pair is separated by a comma. (No comma is specified after the last column.) In this example, columns `cust_name` and `cust_email` will both be updated for customer `10005`.

> TIP: **Using Subqueries in an `UPDATE` Statement**
>
> Subqueries may be used in `UPDATE` statements, enabling you to update columns with data retrieved with a `SELECT` statement. Refer back to Lesson 14, "Working with Subqueries," for more information on subqueries and their uses.

To delete a column's value, you can set it to NULL (assuming the table is defined to allow NULL values). You can do this as follows:

Input ▼

```
UPDATE customers
SET cust_email = NULL
WHERE cust_id = 10005;
```

Here the `NULL` keyword is used to save no value to the `cust_email` column.

Deleting Data

To delete (remove) data from a table, the `DELETE` statement is used. `DELETE` can be used in two ways:

- To delete specific rows from a table
- To delete all rows from a table

You'll now take a look at each of these.

> CAUTION: **Don't Omit the `WHERE` Clause**
>
> Special care must be exercised when using `DELETE` because it is all too easy to mistakenly delete every row from your table. Please read this entire section on `DELETE` before using this statement.

> TIP: **`DELETE` and Security**
>
> Use of the `DELETE` statement can be restricted and controlled. More on this in Lesson 26.

I already stated that `UPDATE` is very easy to use. The good (and bad) news is that `DELETE` is even easier to use.

The following statement deletes a single row from the `customers` table:

Input ▼

```
DELETE FROM customers
WHERE cust_id = 10006;
```

This statement should be self-explanatory. `DELETE FROM` requires that you specify the name of the table from which to delete the data. The `WHERE` clause filters which rows to delete. In this example, only customer `10006` will be deleted. If the `WHERE` clause were omitted, this statement would have deleted every customer in the table.

> NOTE: **No Output**
>
> `DELETE` statements usually generate no output, but if you execute the previous statement in Oracle SQL Developer, you should see a `1 row deleted.` message—and yes, that means that if more than one row was deleted, you probably omitted (or mistyped) the `WHERE` clause.

`DELETE` takes no column names or wildcard characters. `DELETE` deletes entire rows, not columns. To delete specific columns, use an `UPDATE` statement (as shown earlier in this lesson).

> NOTE: **Table Contents, Not Tables**
>
> The DELETE statement deletes rows from tables, even all rows from tables, but DELETE never deletes the table itself.

Guidelines for Updating and Deleting Data

The UPDATE and DELETE statements used in the previous sections all have WHERE clauses, and there is a very good reason for this. If you omit the WHERE clause, the UPDATE or DELETE is applied to every row in the table. In other words, if you execute an UPDATE without a WHERE clause, every row in the table is updated with the new values. Similarly, if you execute DELETE without a WHERE clause, all the contents of the table are deleted.

Here are some best practices that many SQL programmers follow:

- Never execute an UPDATE or a DELETE without a WHERE clause unless you really do intend to update and delete every row.
- Make sure every table has a primary key (refer to Lesson 15, "Joining Tables," if you have forgotten what this is), and use it as the WHERE clause whenever possible. (You may specify individual primary keys, multiple values, or value ranges.)
- Before you use a WHERE clause with an UPDATE or a DELETE, first test it with a SELECT to make sure it is filtering the right records—it is far too easy to write incorrect WHERE clauses.
- Use database-enforced referential integrity (refer to Lesson 15 for this one, too) so Oracle will not allow the deletion of rows that have data in other tables related to them.

> CAUTION: **Use with Caution**
>
> The bottom line is that Oracle has no Undo button. Be very careful using UPDATE and DELETE, or you'll find yourself updating and deleting the wrong data.

Summary

In this lesson, you learned how to use the `UPDATE` and `DELETE` statements to manipulate the data in your tables. You learned the syntax for each of these statements, as well as the inherent dangers they expose. You also learned why `WHERE` clauses are so important in `UPDATE` and `DELETE` statements, and you were given guidelines that should be followed to help ensure that data does not get damaged inadvertently.

LESSON 20

Creating and Manipulating Tables

In this lesson, you'll learn the basics of table creation, alteration, and deletion.

Creating Tables

Oracle PL/SQL statements are not used just for table data manipulation. Indeed, SQL statements can be used to perform all database and table operations, including the creation and manipulation of tables themselves.

There are generally two ways to create database tables:

- Using a database client (like the ones discussed in Lesson 2, "Getting Started with Oracle and PL/SQL") that can be used to create and manage database tables interactively
- Manipulating tables directly with Oracle PL/SQL statements

To create tables programmatically, the `CREATE TABLE` SQL statement is used. It is worth noting that when you use interactive tools, you are actually using Oracle SQL statements. Instead of your writing these statements, however, the interface generates and executes the SQL seamlessly for you (the same is true for changes to existing tables).

> TIP: **Additional Examples**
>
> For additional examples of table creation scripts, see the code used to create the sample tables used in this book.

> NOTE: **Just the Basics**
>
> Oracle supports a vast array of table creation options, far more than a single lesson can do justice to. In this lesson, we cover the basics, just so you can get a feel for what's involved in table creation, and so that the accompanying table creation scripts make sense. To learn more about all that `CREATE TABLE` can do, you'll want to consult the Oracle documentation.

The Basics of Table Creation

To create a table using `CREATE TABLE`, you must specify the following information:

- The name of the new table specified after the keywords `CREATE TABLE`
- The name and definition of the table columns separated by commas

The `CREATE TABLE` statement may also include other keywords and options, but at a minimum you need the table name and column details. The following Oracle SQL statement creates the `customers` table used throughout this book:

Input ▼

```
-----------------------------------------
-- Create customers table
-----------------------------------------
CREATE TABLE customers
(
  cust_id      int       NOT NULL ,
  cust_name    char(50)  NOT NULL ,
  cust_address char(50)  NULL ,
  cust_city    char(50)  NULL ,
  cust_state   char(5)   NULL ,
  cust_zip     char(10)  NULL ,
  cust_country char(50)  NULL ,
  cust_contact char(50)  NULL ,
  cust_email   char(255) NULL
);
```

Analysis ▼

The first few lines in this example are comments, and are thus ignored by Oracle. The new table name is specified immediately following the `CREATE TABLE` keywords. The actual table definition (all the columns) is enclosed within parentheses. The columns themselves are separated by commas. This particular table is made up of nine columns. Each column definition starts with the column name (which must be unique within the table), followed by the column's datatype. (Refer to Lesson 1, "Understanding SQL," for an explanation of datatypes.)

What are not in the previous `CREATE TABLE` statement are the primary and foreign key definitions. Although it is possible to define primary keys at table creation time, the code is often cleaner and easier to maintain when those are added after table creation. We'll revisit this when we introduce `ALTER TABLE` shortly.

> TIP: **Statement Formatting**
>
> As you may recall, white space is ignored in SQL statements. Statements can be typed on one long line or broken up over many lines. It makes no difference at all. This enables you to format your SQL as best suits you. The preceding `CREATE TABLE` statement is a good example of SQL statement formatting—the code is specified over multiple lines, with the column definitions indented for easier reading and editing. Formatting your SQL in this way is entirely optional, but highly recommended.

Working with `NULL` Values

Back in Lesson 6, "Filtering Data," you learned that `NULL` values are no values or the lack of a value. A column that allows `NULL` values also allows rows to be inserted with no value at all in that column. A column that does not allow `NULL` values does not accept rows with no value—in other words, that column will always be required when rows are inserted or updated.

Every table column is either a `NULL` column or a `NOT NULL` column, and that state is specified in the table definition at creation time. Take a look at the following example:

Input ▼

```
-----------------------------------------
-- Create orders table
-----------------------------------------
CREATE TABLE orders
(
  order_num  int  NOT NULL ,
  order_date date NOT NULL ,
  cust_id    int  NOT NULL
);
```

Analysis ▼

This statement creates the `orders` table used throughout this book. `orders` contains three columns: order number, order date, and the customer ID. All three columns are required, and so each contains the keyword NOT NULL. This prevents the insertion of columns with no value. If someone tries to insert no value, an error will be returned, and the insertion will fail.

This next example creates a table with a mixture of NULL and NOT NULL columns:

Input ▼

```
-----------------------------------------
-- Create vendors table
-----------------------------------------
CREATE TABLE vendors
(
  vend_id       int      NOT NULL,
  vend_name     char(50) NOT NULL ,
  vend_address  char(50) NULL ,
  vend_city     char(50) NULL ,
  vend_state    char(5)  NULL ,
  vend_zip      char(10) NULL ,
  vend_country  char(50) NULL
);
```

Analysis ▼

This statement creates the `vendors` table used throughout this book. The vendor ID and vendor name columns are both required, and are, therefore, specified as `NOT NULL`. The five remaining columns all allow `NULL` values, and so `NOT NULL` is not specified. `NULL` is the default setting, so if `NOT NULL` is not specified, `NULL` is assumed.

> CAUTION: **Understanding** `NULL`
>
> Don't confuse `NULL` values with empty strings. A `NULL` value is the lack of a value; it is not an empty string. If you were to specify `''` (two single quotes with nothing in between them), that would be allowed in a `NOT NULL` column. An empty string is a valid value; it is not no value. `NULL` values are specified with the keyword `NULL`, not with an empty string.

Specifying Default Values

Oracle allows you to specify default values to be used if no value is specified when a row is inserted. Default values are specified using the `DEFAULT` keyword in the column definitions in the `CREATE TABLE` statement.

Look at the following example (not the one we actually use in this book):

Input ▼

```
---------------------------------------------
-- Create orderitems table
---------------------------------------------
CREATE TABLE orderitems
(
  order_num  int           NOT NULL ,
  order_item int           NOT NULL ,
  prod_id    char(10)      NOT NULL ,
  quantity   int           DEFAULT 1 NOT NULL ,
  item_price decimal(8,2)  NOT NULL
);
```

Analysis ▼

This statement creates the `orderitems` table that contains the individual items that make up an order. (The order itself is stored in the `orders` table.) The `quantity` column contains the quantity for each item in an order. In this example, adding the text `DEFAULT 1` to the column description instructs Oracle to use a quantity of `1` if no quantity is specified.

> TIP: **Using `DEFAULT` Instead of `NULL` Values**
>
> Many database developers use `DEFAULT` values instead of `NULL` columns, especially in columns that will be used in calculations or data groupings.

Updating Tables

To update table definitions, the `ALTER TABLE` statement is used, but ideally, tables should never be altered after they contain data. You should spend sufficient time anticipating future needs during the table design process so extensive changes are not required later on.

To change a table using `ALTER TABLE`, you must specify the following information:

- The name of the table to be altered after the keywords `ALTER TABLE`. (The table must exist or an error will be generated.)
- The list of changes to be made.

The following example adds a column to a table:

Input ▼

```
ALTER TABLE vendors
ADD vend_phone CHAR(20);
```

Analysis ▼

This statement adds a column named `vend_phone` to the `vendors` table. The datatype must be specified.

To remove this newly added column, you can do the following:

Input ▼

```
ALTER TABLE vendors
DROP COLUMN vend_phone;
```

Primary Keys Revisited

As already explained, primary key values must be unique. That is, every row in a table must have a unique primary key value. If a single column is used for the primary key, it must be unique; if multiple columns are used, the combination of them must be unique.

Primary keys can be defined within `CREATE TABLE` statements. However, many developers prefer to create their tables and then add all keys. Adding keys is a table update, and so the `ALTER TABLE` command is used.

Here's an example:

Input ▼

```
----------------------
-- Define primary keys
----------------------
ALTER TABLE customers ADD CONSTRAINT pk_customers
                      PRIMARY KEY (cust_id);
ALTER TABLE orderitems ADD CONSTRAINT pk_orderitems
                       PRIMARY KEY (order_num, order_item);
ALTER TABLE orders ADD CONSTRAINT pk_orders
                   PRIMARY KEY (order_num);
ALTER TABLE products ADD CONSTRAINT pk_products
                     PRIMARY KEY (prod_id);
ALTER TABLE vendors ADD CONSTRAINT pk_vendors
                    PRIMARY KEY (vend_id);
ALTER TABLE productnotes ADD CONSTRAINT pk_productnotes
                         PRIMARY KEY (note_id);
```

Analysis ▼

The preceding block of code is from our `create.sql` file, and it defines the primary keys for all six tables. `ALTER TABLE` is used to update a table, and ADD CONSTRAINT PRIMARY KEY specifies that the table change is the addition of a primary key. All keys must be named with unique names; here I used pk_ followed by the table name. Finally, the column (or columns) that comprise the primary key are identified.

Defining Foreign Keys

ALTER TABLE is also used to define foreign keys. The following is the code used to define the foreign keys used by the tables in this book:

Input ▼

```
---------------------------------------------
-- Define foreign keys
---------------------------------------------
ALTER TABLE orderitems
      ADD CONSTRAINT fk_orderitems_orders FOREIGN KEY (order_
➥num)
      REFERENCES orders (order_num);
ALTER TABLE orderitems
      ADD CONSTRAINT fk_orderitems_products
      FOREIGN KEY (prod_id) REFERENCES products (prod_id);
ALTER TABLE orders
      ADD CONSTRAINT fk_orders_customers FOREIGN KEY (cust_id)
      REFERENCES customers (cust_id);
ALTER TABLE products
      ADD CONSTRAINT fk_products_vendors
      FOREIGN KEY (vend_id) REFERENCES vendors (vend_id);
ALTER TABLE productnotes
      ADD CONSTRAINT fk_productnotes_products
      FOREIGN KEY (prod_id) REFERENCES products (prod_id);
```

Analysis ▼

Here five ALTER TABLE statements are used, because five different tables are being altered. As we did when the primary keys were defined, ADD CONSTRAINT is used this time specifying FOREIGN KEY, the constraint is named, and the impacted table is defined. Because this is a foreign key, we also need to define the table and column that it is dependent on, and that gets passed to REFERENCES. REFERENCES customers (cust_id) means that the only values in this column are ones in the cust_id column in the customers table.

To make multiple alterations to a single table, a single `ALTER TABLE` statement could be used with each of the alterations specified and delimited by commas.

> CAUTION: **Use `ALTER TABLE` Carefully**
>
> Use `ALTER TABLE` with extreme caution, and be sure you have a complete set of backups (both schema and data) before proceeding. Database table changes cannot be undone—and if you add columns you don't need, you might not be able to remove them. Similarly, if you drop a column that you do need, you might lose all the data in that column.

Deleting Tables

Deleting tables (actually removing the entire table, not just the contents) is very easy—arguably too easy. Tables are deleted using the `DROP TABLE` statement:

Input ▼

```
DROP TABLE customers2;
```

Analysis ▼

This statement deletes the `customers2` table (assuming it exists). There is no confirmation, nor is there an undo—executing the statement permanently removes the table.

Renaming Tables

To rename a table, use the `ALTER TABLE` statement as follows:

Input ▼

```
ALTER TABLE customers2 RENAME TO customers;
```

Analysis ▼

`RENAME TABLE` does just that—it renames a table.

Summary

In this lesson, you learned several new SQL statements. `CREATE TABLE` is used to create new tables, `ALTER TABLE` is used to change table columns (or other objects like constraints or indexes), and `DROP TABLE` is used to completely delete a table. These statements should be used with extreme caution, and only after backups have been made. You also learned about database engines, defining primary and foreign keys, and other important table and column options.

LESSON 21

Using Views

In this lesson, you'll learn exactly what views are, how they work, and when they should be used. You'll also see how views can be used to simplify some of the SQL operations performed in earlier lessons.

Understanding Views

Views are virtual tables. Unlike tables that contain data, views simply contain queries that dynamically retrieve data when used.

The best way to understand views is to look at an example. Back in Lesson 15, "Joining Tables," you used the following SELECT statement to retrieve data from three tables:

Input ▼

```
SELECT cust_name, cust_contact
FROM customers, orders, orderitems
WHERE customers.cust_id = orders.cust_id
  AND orderitems.order_num = orders.order_num
  AND prod_id = 'TNT2';
```

That query was used to retrieve the customers who had ordered a specific product. Anyone needing this data would have to understand the table structure, as well as how to create the query and join the tables. To retrieve the same data for another product (or for multiple products), the last WHERE clause would have to be modified.

Now imagine that you could wrap that entire query in a virtual table called productcustomers. You could then simply do the following to retrieve the same data:

Input ▼

```
SELECT cust_name, cust_contact
FROM productcustomers
WHERE prod_id = 'TNT2';
```

This is where views come into play. `productcustomers` is a view, and as a view, it does not contain any actual columns or data as a table would. Instead, it contains a SQL query—the same query used previously to join the tables properly.

Why Use Views

You've already seen one use for views. Here are some other common uses:

- To reuse SQL statements.
- To simplify complex SQL operations. After the query is written, it can be reused easily, without your having to know the details of the underlying query itself.
- To expose parts of a table instead of complete tables.
- To secure data. Users can be given access to specific subsets of tables instead of to entire tables.
- To change data formatting and representation. Views can return data formatted and presented differently from their underlying tables.

For the most part, after views are created, they can be used in the same way as tables. You can perform `SELECT` operations, filter and sort data, join views to other views or tables, and possibly even add and update data. (There are some restrictions on this last item. More on that in a moment.)

The important thing to remember is views are just that—views into data stored elsewhere. Views contain no data themselves, so the data they return is retrieved from other tables. When data is added or changed in those tables, the views return that changed data.

> CAUTION: **Performance Issues**
>
> Because views contain no data, any retrieval needed to execute a query must be processed every time the view is used. If you create complex views with multiple joins and filters, or if you nest views, you may find that performance is dramatically degraded. Be sure you test execution before deploying applications that use views extensively.

View Rules and Restrictions

Here are some of the most common rules and restrictions governing view creation and usage:

- Like tables, views must be uniquely named. (They cannot be named with the name of any other table or view.)
- There is no limit to the number of views that can be created.
- To create views, you must have security access. This is usually granted by the database administrator.
- Views can be nested; that is, a view may be built using a query that retrieves data from another view.
- `ORDER BY` may be used in a view, but it will be overridden if `ORDER BY` is also used in the `SELECT` that retrieves data from the view.
- Views cannot be indexed, nor can they have triggers or default values associated with them.
- Views can be used in conjunction with tables; for example, to create a `SELECT` statement which joins a table and a view.

Using Views

So now that you know what views are (and the rules and restrictions that govern them), let's look at view creation:

- Views are created using the `CREATE VIEW` statement.
- To remove a view, the `DROP` statement is used. The syntax is simply `DROP VIEW viewname;`.

- To update a view, you may use the `DROP` statement and then the `CREATE` statement again, or just use `CREATE OR REPLACE VIEW`, which creates it if it does not exist and replace it if it does.

Using Views to Simplify Complex Joins

One of the most common uses of views is to hide complex SQL, and this often involves joins. Look at the following statement:

Input ▼

```
CREATE VIEW productcustomers AS
SELECT cust_name, cust_contact, prod_id
FROM customers, orders, orderitems
WHERE customers.cust_id = orders.cust_id
  AND orderitems.order_num = orders.order_num;
```

> NOTE: **No Output**
>
> `CREATE VIEW` statements generate no output, but if you execute the preceding statement in Oracle SQL Developer, you should see a `view PRODUCTCUSTOMERS created` message.

Analysis ▼

This statement creates a view named `productcustomers`, which joins three tables to return a list of all customers who have ordered any product. If you were to `SELECT * FROM productcustomers`, you would list every customer who ordered anything.

To retrieve a list of customers who ordered product `TNT2`, you can do the following:

Input ▼

```
SELECT cust_name, cust_contact
FROM productcustomers
WHERE prod_id = 'TNT2';
```

Output ▼

```
+-----------------+---------------+
| cust_name       | cust_contact  |
+-----------------+---------------+
| Coyote Inc.     | Y Lee         |
| Yosemite Place  | Y Sam         |
+-----------------+---------------+
```

Analysis ▼

This statement retrieves specific data from the view by issuing a `WHERE` clause. When Oracle processes the request, it adds the specified `WHERE` clause to any existing `WHERE` clauses in the view query so the data is filtered correctly.

As you can see, views can be used in `SELECT` statements just like any other tables. Using them can greatly simplify the use of complex SQL statements. Using views, you can write the underlying SQL once and then reuse it as needed.

> TIP: **Creating Reusable Views**
>
> It is a good idea to create views that are not tied to specific data. For example, the view created in this example returns customers for all products, not just product `TNT2` (for which the view was first created). Expanding the scope of the view enables it to be reused, making it even more useful. It also eliminates the need for you to create and maintain multiple similar views.

Using Views to Reformat Retrieved Data

As mentioned previously, another common use of views is for reformatting retrieved data. The following `SELECT` statement (from Lesson 10, "Creating Calculated Fields") returns vendor name and location in a single combined calculated column:

Input ▼

```
SELECT RTrim(vend_name) || ', (' || RTrim(vend_country) || ')'
➥AS vend_title
FROM vendors
ORDER BY vend_name;
```

Output ▼

```
+-------------------------+
| vend_title              |
+-------------------------+
| ACME (USA)              |
| Anvils R Us (USA)       |
| Furball Inc. (USA)      |
| Jet Set (England)       |
| Jouets Et Ours (France) |
| LT Supplies (USA)       |
+-------------------------+
```

Now suppose that you regularly needed results in this format. Rather than perform the concatenation each time it was needed, you could create a view and use that instead. To turn this statement into a view, you can do the following:

Input ▼

```
CREATE VIEW vendorlocations AS
SELECT RTrim(vend_name) || ' (' || RTrim(vend_country) || ')'
➥AS vend_title
FROM vendors
ORDER BY vend_name;
```

Analysis ▼

This statement creates a view using the exact same query as the previous SELECT statement. To retrieve the data to create all mailing labels, simply do the following:

Input ▼

```
SELECT *
FROM vendorlocations;
```

Output ▼

```
+-------------------------+
| vend_title              |
+-------------------------+
| ACME (USA)              |
| Anvils R Us (USA)       |
| Furball Inc. (USA)      |
| Jet Set (England)       |
| Jouets Et Ours (France) |
| LT Supplies (USA)       |
+-------------------------+
```

Using Views to Filter Unwanted Data

Views are also useful for applying common `WHERE` clauses. For example, you might want to define a `customeremaillist` view so it filters out customers without email addresses. To do this, you can use the following statement:

Input ▼

```
CREATE VIEW customeremaillist AS
SELECT cust_id, cust_name, cust_email
FROM customers
WHERE cust_email IS NOT NULL;
```

Analysis ▼

Obviously, when sending email to a mailing list, you want to ignore users who have no email address. The `WHERE` clause here filters out those rows that have `NULL` values in the `cust_email` columns so they won't be retrieved.

View `customeremaillist` can now be used for data retrieval just like any table.

Input ▼

```
SELECT *
FROM customeremaillist;
```

Output ▼

```
+----------+---------------+--------------------+
| cust_id  | cust_name     | cust_email         |
+----------+---------------+--------------------+
|   10001  | Coyote Inc.   | ylee@coyote.com    |
|   10003  | Wascals       | rabbit@wascally.com |
|   10004  | Yosemite Place | sam@yosemite.com  |
+----------+---------------+--------------------+
```

> NOTE: `WHERE` **Clauses and** `WHERE` **Clauses**
>
> If a `WHERE` clause is used when retrieving data from the view, the two sets of clauses (the one in the view and the one passed to it) will be combined automatically.

Using Views with Calculated Fields

Views are exceptionally useful for simplifying the use of calculated fields. The following is a `SELECT` statement introduced in Lesson 10. It retrieves the order items for a specific order, calculating the expanded price for each item:

Input ▼

```
SELECT prod_id,
       quantity,
       item_price,
       quantity*item_price AS expanded_price
FROM orderitems
WHERE order_num = 20005;
```

Output ▼

```
+---------+----------+------------+----------------+
| prod_id | quantity | item_price | expanded_price |
+---------+----------+------------+----------------+
| ANV01   |       10 |   5.99     | 59.90          |
| ANV02   |        3 |   9.99     | 29.97          |
| TNT2    |        5 |     10     |    50          |
| FB      |        1 |     10     |    10          |
+---------+----------+------------+----------------+
```

To create a view that can return the same data for any order, do the following:

Input ▼

```
CREATE VIEW orderitemsexpanded AS
SELECT order_num,
       prod_id,
       quantity,
       item_price,
       quantity*item_price AS expanded_price
FROM orderitems;
```

To retrieve the details for order `20005` (the previous output), do the following:

Input ▼

```
SELECT *
FROM orderitemsexpanded
WHERE order_num = 20005;
```

Output ▼

```
+-----------+---------+----------+------------+----------------+
| order_num | prod_id | quantity | item_price | expanded_price |
+-----------+---------+----------+------------+----------------+
|     20005 | ANV01   |       10 |       5.99 |           59.9 |
|     20005 | ANV02   |        3 |       9.99 |          29.97 |
|     20005 | TNT2    |        5 |         10 |             50 |
|     20005 | FB      |        1 |         10 |             10 |
+-----------+---------+----------+------------+----------------+
```

As you can see, views are easy to create and even easier to use. Used correctly, views can greatly simplify complex data manipulation.

Updating Views

All the views thus far have been used with `SELECT` statements. But can view data be updated? The answer is that it depends.

As a rule, yes, views are updateable (that is, you can use `INSERT`, `UPDATE`, and `DELETE` on them). Updating a view updates the underlying table (the view, if you recall, has no data of its own); if you add or remove rows from a view, you are actually removing them from the underlying table.

However, not all views are updateable. Basically, if Oracle is unable to correctly ascertain the underlying data to be updated, updates (this includes inserts and deletes) are not allowed. In practice, this means that if any of the following are used, you'll not be able to update the view:

- Grouping (using `GROUP BY` and `HAVING`)
- Joins
- Subqueries
- Unions
- Aggregate functions (`Min()`, `Count()`, `Sum()`, and so forth)
- `DISTINCT`
- Derived (calculated) columns

In other words, many of the examples used in this lesson would not be updateable. This might sounds like a serious restriction, but in reality it isn't because views are primarily used for data retrieval anyway.

> TIP: **Use Views for Retrieval**
>
> As a rule, use views for data retrieval (`SELECT` statements) and not for updates (`INSERT`, `UPDATE`, and `DELETE`).

Summary

Views are virtual tables. They do not contain data, but they contain queries that retrieve data as needed, instead. Views provide a level of encapsulation around Oracle `SELECT` statements and can be used to simplify data manipulation, as well as to reformat or secure underlying data.

LESSON 22
Working with Stored Procedures

In this lesson, you'll learn what stored procedures are, why they are used, and how they are used. You'll also look at the basic syntax for creating and using them.

Understanding Stored Procedures

Most of the SQL statements that we've used thus far are simple in that they use a single statement against one or more tables. Not all operations are that simple—often, multiple statements are needed to perform a complete operation. For example, consider the following scenario:

- To process an order, checks must be made to ensure that items are in stock.
- If items are in stock, they need to be reserved so they are not sold to anyone else, and the available quantity must be reduced to reflect the correct amount in stock.
- Any items not in stock need to be ordered; this requires some interaction with the vendor.
- The customer needs to be notified as to which items are in stock (and can be shipped immediately) and which are back ordered.

This is obviously not a complete example, and it is even beyond the scope of the example tables that we have been using in this book, but it suffices to help make a point. Performing this process requires many PL/SQL statements against many tables. In addition, the exact statements that need to be performed and their order are not fixed; they can (and will) vary according to which items are in stock and which are not.

How would you write this code? You could write each of the statements individually and execute other statements conditionally, based on the result. You would have to do this every time this processing was needed (and in every application that needed it).

You could also create a stored procedure. *Stored procedures* are simply collections of one or more Oracle PL/SQL statements saved for future use. You can think of them as batch files, although in truth they are more than that.

The language used to write stored procedures in Oracle is PL/SQL, and the PL is important, because it's the procedural language that provides everything from if statements to loops and more.

> NOTE: **Just an Introduction**
>
> Oracle stored procedures are powerful and capable, and there's a lot to learn and master. There are entire books, books far bigger than this one, just on the subject. This lesson is not going to teach you all you need to know about functions and stored procedures. Rather, I want to use this lesson to help you understand what they are, what they look like, and what they can do. Then, when you run into an opportunity that calls for one, you'll know which direction to head in.

Why Use Stored Procedures

Now that you know what stored procedures are, why use them? There are many reasons, but here are the primary ones:

- To simplify complex operations (as shown in the previous example) by encapsulating processes into a single easy-to-use unit.
- To ensure data integrity by not requiring that a series of steps be created over and over. If all developers and applications use the same (tried-and-tested) stored procedure, the same code will be used by all.

  An extension of this concept is to prevent errors. The more steps that must be performed, the more likely it is that errors will be introduced. Preventing errors ensures data consistency.

- To simplify change management. If tables, column names, or business logic (or just about anything) changes, only the stored procedure code needs to be updated, and no one else needs even to be aware that changes were made.

  An extension of this concept is security. Restricting access to underlying data via stored procedures reduces the chance of data corruption (unintentional or otherwise).

- To improve performance, because stored procedures typically execute quicker than individual SQL statements do.

In other words, there are three primary benefits—simplicity, security, and performance. Obviously all are extremely important. Before you run off to turn all your SQL code into stored procedures, here are the downsides:

- Stored procedures tend to be more complex to write than basic SQL statements, and writing them requires a greater degree of skill and experience.
- You might not have the security access needed to create stored procedures. Many database administrators restrict stored procedure creation rights, allowing users to execute them but not necessarily create them.

Nonetheless, stored procedures are very useful and should be used whenever possible.

Using Stored Procedures

We're going to look at several stored procedures, increasing in sophistication and complexity as we go.

> NOTE: **What About Functions?**
>
> In addition to stored procedures, Oracle also supports functions. Functions and stored procedures are very similar; they allow you to encapsulate blocks of functionality. The main difference between functions and stored procedures is in what they return: Functions always return a single value (much like the

SQL functions we've been using throughout this book). Stored procedures don't return values, but they do accept parameters that can be used to pass data both in and out. Within the body of functions and stored procedures, the code you can write and the operations you can perform are much the same. The difference is in how the code will be used and executed. As such, what you'll learn here also applies to functions, even though we don't focus on them explicitly.

Basic Stored Procedure Syntax

We'll start with a simple example—the Oracle stored procedure equivalent of Hello World. Here's the code:

Input ▼

```
CREATE OR REPLACE PROCEDURE Hello IS
BEGIN
DBMS_OUTPUT.PUT_LINE('Hello World');
END;
```

Analysis ▼

Stored procedures are created using the `CREATE PROCEDURE` statement, and here the procedure is named `Hello`. The body of a stored procedure is placed between `BEGIN` and `END` statements, and the body of this stored procedure simply displays `Hello World` in the output window.

TIP: **Use** `CREATE OR REPLACE`

To update a stored procedure, you must delete it and then create it again. Or, instead of using `CREATE PROCEDURE`, use `CREATE OR REPLACE PROCEDURE` as we did here. This way if the stored procedure doesn't exist it'll be created, but if it does exist it'll be updated.

So how do you execute this stored procedure? You use the `EXECUTE` statement, like this:

Input ▼

```
EXECUTE Hello
```

Output ▼

```
Hello World
```

Analysis ▼

`EXECUTE` does just that—it executes a stored procedure, which in this case simply displays `Hello World`. Okay, so that's a bit anti-climactic, but it'll get better in a moment.

Using Programming Constructs in Stored Procedures

Things become a little more interesting when stored procedures employ programming constructs. Here's an example:

Input ▼

```
CREATE OR REPLACE PROCEDURE Greeting IS

h number;
g char(20);

BEGIN

SELECT EXTRACT(HOUR FROM CURRENT_TIMESTAMP) INTO h FROM dual;

IF h >= 20 OR h <= 5 THEN
  g := 'Goodnight!';
ELSIF h > 5 AND h <= 12 THEN
  g := 'Good morning!';
ELSIF h > 12 AND h <= 17 THEN
  g := 'Good afternoon!';
ELSE
  g := 'Good evening!';
END IF;

DBMS_OUTPUT.PUT_LINE(g);
END;
```

Analysis ▼

This stored procedure displays `Good morning!`, `Good afternoon!`, `Good evening!`, or `Goodnight!` depending on the time of day. As in the previous example, `CREATE OR REPLACE PROCEDURE` is used to create a procedure, this time named `Greeting`. Next, two variables are created, `h` (a number) to hold the current hour, and `g` (text) to hold the greeting text. `BEGIN` starts the body, a `SELECT` statement obtains the current system hour, and `INTO h` tells the `SELECT` to save the result in variable `h`. Next comes an `IF` block that simply looks at the hour and saves an appropriate greeting into variable `g`. Finally, `g` is displayed (just like we displayed `Hello World` previously).

To run this stored procedure, just do the following:

Input ▼

```
EXECUTE Greeting
```

Building Intelligent Stored Procedures

Now that you've seen some of what stored procedures can do, let's look at a more useful example, one that solves an actual business problem. Back in Lesson 18, "Inserting Data," you learned how to add rows to a table. For our example, we added a customer, and you had to make sure that the customer was assigned a new and unique id; otherwise, a key constraint error would be thrown. Therefore, you had to pick a new number yourself, making sure that it was not already in use. Obviously, in the real world, you would not want to ask users to do this. Customer id assignment should happen safely, reliably, and automatically.

This next stored procedure demonstrates one way to accomplish this. Rather than use `INSERT` to add a customer, you can create a stored procedure that does the insertion for you. You simply pass it the customer info, and it finds the next available id to use and then inserts the new customer.

Here's the code:

Input ▼

```
-- Add a new customer
CREATE OR REPLACE PROCEDURE CustomerAdd(
    v_cust_name IN customers.cust_name%TYPE,
    v_cust_address IN customers.cust_address%TYPE,
    v_cust_city IN customers.cust_city%TYPE,
    v_cust_state IN customers.cust_state%TYPE,
    v_cust_zip IN customers.cust_zip%TYPE,
    v_cust_country IN customers.cust_country%TYPE,
    v_cust_contact IN customers.cust_contact%TYPE,
    v_cust_email IN customers.cust_email%TYPE)
IS

-- Variable for customer id
v_cust_id number;

BEGIN

-- Get current highest customer id
SELECT MAX(cust_id) INTO v_cust_id
FROM customers;

-- Increment customer id
v_cust_id := v_cust_id+1;

-- Insert new customer
 INSERT INTO customers(cust_id,
                       cust_name,
                       cust_address,
                       cust_city,
                       cust_state,
                       cust_zip,
                       cust_country,
                       cust_contact,
                       cust_email)
 VALUES(v_cust_id,
        v_cust_name,
        v_cust_address,
        v_cust_city,
        v_cust_state,
        v_cust_zip,
        v_cust_country,
        v_cust_contact,
        v_cust_email);
```

```
    COMMIT;

END;
```

Analysis ▼

This example is more complicated, so I've added comments (something you should always do in all of your stored procedures). Once again, `CREATE OR REPLACE PROCEDURE` is used to create a stored procedure named `CustomerAdd`. This stored procedure needs to accept customer data, and each piece of data is specified as a parameter to the stored procedure.

Because eight pieces of data must be passed in, there are eight parameters defined, the first of which is `v_cust_name IN customers.cust_name%TYPE`. The first part of the parameter definition creates a variable named `v_cust_name` (I like to name my variables `v_` followed by the associated table column). `IN` specifies that this parameter is being used to pass data into the stored procedure (as opposed to `OUT` of it). `customers.cust_name%TYPE` specifies that this parameter is associated with the `cust_name` column in the `customers` table. This same pattern is repeated for all eight parameters.

Next, the code creates a variable to store the customer id we'll be using.

`BEGIN` starts the stored procedure body, and the first thing we need to do is to determine the current highest customer id. As you might recall from Lesson 12, "Summarizing Data," `MAX()` can find the greatest value in a column, and so we `SELECT MAX(cust_id)` from the `customers` table, and save it `INTO v_cust_id`. Now variable `v_cust_id` contains the current highest customer id, but we need a value greater than that, and so `v_cust_id := v_cust_id+1;` increments `v_cust_id` by 1.

Next comes the `INSERT` statement, which is just like the one you saw in Lesson 18, except that this time the `VALUES` are all variables, a local variable for `cust_id`, and the passed parameters for all the others.

Finally, `COMMIT` is used to save the changes, and the stored procedure is closed with `END;`.

To try this example, use the following EXECUTE statement:

Input ▼

```
EXECUTE CustomerAdd('Pep E. LaPew',
                    '100 Main Street',
                    'Los Angeles',
                    'CA',
                    '90046',
                    'USA',
                    NULL,
                    NULL)
```

Analysis ▼

By now, the code should be self-explanatory. EXECUTE runs the stored procedure, and all necessary values are passed as parameters. The stored procedure then defines a new customer id, and INSERTS the new customer.

Dropping Stored Procedures

After they are created, stored procedures remain on the server, ready for use, until dropped. The DROP command (similar to the statement shown in Lesson 20, "Creating and Manipulating Tables") removes the stored procedure from the server.

To remove the stored procedure we just created, use the following statement:

Input ▼

```
DROP PROCEDURE Greeting;
```

Analysis ▼

This removes the recently created stored procedure.

Summary

In this lesson, you learned what stored procedures are and why they are used. You also learned the basics of stored procedure execution and creation syntax, and you saw some of the ways these can be used. We'll continue this subject in the next lesson.

LESSON 23
Using Cursors

In this lesson, you'll learn what cursors are and how to use them.

Understanding Cursors

As you have seen in previous lessons, Oracle retrieval operations work with sets of rows known as *result sets*. The rows returned are all the rows that match a SQL statement—zero or more of them. Using simple `SELECT` statements, there is no way to get the first row, the next row, or the previous 10 rows, for example. Nor is there an easy way to process all rows, one at a time (as opposed to all of them in a batch).

Sometimes you need to step through rows forward or backward and one or more at a time. This is what cursors are used for. A *cursor* is a database query stored on the Oracle server—not a `SELECT` statement, but the result set retrieved by that statement. After the cursor is stored, applications can scroll or browse up and down through the data as needed.

To help demonstrate this, consider the following scenario. Our `vendors` table contains vendor names and addresses. In the real world, address data can become inconsistent very quickly; some users might capitalize streets and others might not, some might enter `Rd` and others `Rd.` and yet other `Road`; state and province names might be capitalized or not (or worse, might be mixed case); UK and Canadian style postal codes might have spaces in them or not; and so on. Cleaning up the data to ensure uniformity and consistency is too complex a task for a SQL `UPDATE` statement; converting a column to uppercase for all (or some) rows is easy enough, but applying different rules based on country, for example, requires that each row be processed individually. This is a great task for cursors.

> NOTE: **Explicit and Implicit Cursors**
>
> In Oracle, every time you execute a SQL statement, a cursor is created internally; that's how Oracle itself process the SQL statement. This type of cursor is called an *implicit cursor*, as opposed to the *explicit cursor*, which, as its name suggests, is one you explicitly create. When you work with cursors, you will almost exclusively be using explicit cursors, and so all the examples in this lesson are exactly that. However, although they are not covered in this lesson, if needed, you can work with the implicit cursors that Oracle creates, and the techniques discussed here apply equally to all cursors.

Working with Cursors

Using cursors involves several distinct steps:

1. Before a cursor can be used, it must be declared (defined). This process does not actually retrieve any data; it merely defines the `SELECT` statement to be used.
2. After it is declared, the cursor must be opened for use. This process actually retrieves the data using the previously defined `SELECT` statement.
3. With the cursor populated with data, individual rows can be fetched (retrieved) as needed.
4. When it is done, the cursor must be closed.

Creating Cursors

Cursors are created using the `DECLARE CURSOR` statement. `CURSOR` names the cursor and takes a `SELECT` statement, complete with `WHERE` and other clauses if needed. For example, this statement defines a cursor named `ordernumbers` using a `SELECT` statement that retrieves all orders:

Input ▼

```
DECLARE
   CURSOR c_vendors IS
   SELECT vend_id, vend_name, vend_address,
          vend_city, vend_state, vend_zip, vend_country
   FROM vendors;
```

Analysis ▼

Don't run this code yet; it's not complete enough for Oracle and will generate errors, but let's look at it. `DECLARE CURSOR` does just what its name implies—it creates a new cursor, here named `c_vendors`. The only code in the cursor is a `SELECT` statement, which defines the data that will be used within the cursor.

Now that the cursor is defined, it is ready to be opened.

Opening and Closing Cursors

Cursors are opened using the `OPEN` statement, like this:

Input ▼

```
OPEN c_vendors;
```

After cursor processing is complete, the cursor should be closed using the `CLOSE` statement, as follows:

Input ▼

```
CLOSE c_vendors;
```

Here is a more complete example, and this one runs without any errors:

Input ▼

```
DECLARE
   CURSOR c_vendors IS
   SELECT vend_id, vend_name, vend_address,
          vend_city, vend_state, vend_zip, vend_country
   FROM vendors;
```

```
BEGIN

  OPEN c_vendors;
  CLOSE c_vendors;

END;
```

Analysis ▼

Here, the cursor is defined, it is then opened, and right away closed, but nothing is done with the retrieved data.

Fetching Cursor Data

After a cursor is opened, each row can be accessed individually using a `FETCH` statement. `FETCH` specifies what is to be retrieved (the desired columns) and where retrieved data should be stored. It also advances the internal row pointer within the cursor so the next `FETCH` statement retrieves the next row (and not the same one over and over).

Here's an update to our prior cursor:

Input ▼

```
DECLARE
   -- Declare variables
   v_vend_id vendors.vend_id%TYPE;
   v_vend_name vendors.vend_name%TYPE;
   v_vend_address vendors.vend_address%TYPE;
   v_vend_city vendors.vend_city%TYPE;
   v_vend_state vendors.vend_state%TYPE;
   v_vend_zip vendors.vend_zip%TYPE;
   v_vend_country vendors.vend_country%TYPE;

   -- Declare cursor
   CURSOR c_vendors IS
   SELECT vend_id, vend_name, vend_address,
          vend_city, vend_state, vend_zip, vend_country
   FROM vendors;

BEGIN

  -- Open cursor
  OPEN c_vendors;
```

```
   -- Loop through cursor
   LOOP

      -- Get a row
      FETCH c_vendors INTO v_vend_id,
                           v_vend_name,
                           v_vend_address,
                           v_vend_city,
                           v_vend_state,
                           v_vend_zip,
                           v_vend_country;

      -- When no more rows, exit
      EXIT WHEN c_vendors%notfound;

   END LOOP;

   -- Close cursor
   CLOSE c_vendors;

END;
```

> TIP: **It's PL/SQL**
>
> If the basic code and structure of this cursor looks familiar, that's because it's written in PL/SQL, the same language used in Lesson 22, "Working with Stored Procedures," when we looked at stored procedures. The more you learn about the PL (procedural language) part of PL/SQL, the more you can take advantage of Oracle's more advanced functionality.

Analysis ▼

The cursor has gotten far more complex, so let's walk through it. (Notice that I have commented the code, something that I recommend you always do.)

Once again, we start with a DECLARE statement, but this time it is doing more than declare the cursor; it's also declaring a series of variables that are needed to contain retrieved data (more on that in a moment). The variables are defined in much the same way as we defined stored procedure parameters—they are named, and then associated with specific table columns.

Next comes the cursor definition itself, just as we saw in "Creating Cursors" previously, and the cursor is then opened.

New to this example is the `LOOP` instruction, which defines a block of code that gets repeated. Everything between `LOOP` and `END LOOP` gets repeated over and over, until something within the loop forces an exit.

`FETCH` is then used to fetch one row from the cursor `INTO` specified variables. You'll notice that column names are not specified, and so cursor column order is important. The first column defined in the cursor's `SELECT` statement will be stored in the first variable, the second in the second, and so on. This is why I like to name my variables `v_` (for variable) followed by the name of the column with which they'll be used; it makes working with them a whole lot easier.

`FETCH` fetches one row at a time, and so each time through the loop, a different row is fetched, and the variables are updated with new values. So how does the loop ever terminate? That's what `EXIT` does—it exits the loop, terminating loop processing. You can use `EXIT` any time; you could have put it at the top of the loop and the loop would then immediately terminate. Here we use `EXIT WHEN c_vendors%notfound`, which tells Oracle to `EXIT WHEN` the `c_vendors` cursor returns a `notfound` state indicating that no more rows are left to `FETCH`.

Our cursor isn't actually doing anything with the fetched data, but it is looping through retrieved rows and storing columns into variables.

Using Cursor Data

Now that we can `FETCH` one row at a time, we can work with that data. Look at this next example:

Input ▼

```
DECLARE
   -- Declare variables
   v_vend_id vendors.vend_id%TYPE;
   v_vend_name vendors.vend_name%TYPE;
   v_vend_address vendors.vend_address%TYPE;
   v_vend_city vendors.vend_city%TYPE;
   v_vend_state vendors.vend_state%TYPE;
```

```
  v_vend_zip vendors.vend_zip%TYPE;
  v_vend_country vendors.vend_country%TYPE;

  -- Declare cursor
  CURSOR c_vendors IS
  SELECT vend_id, vend_name, vend_address,
         vend_city, vend_state, vend_zip, vend_country
  FROM vendors;

BEGIN

 -- Open cursor
 OPEN c_vendors;

 -- Loop through cursor
 LOOP

   -- Get a row
   FETCH c_vendors INTO v_vend_id,
                        v_vend_name,
                        v_vend_address,
                        v_vend_city,
                        v_vend_state,
                        v_vend_zip,
                        v_vend_country;

      -- Is this address in USA?
      IF Trim(v_vend_country) = 'USA' THEN
        -- Make sure state abbreviation is upper case
        v_vend_state := Upper(v_vend_state);
        -- Update the vendor
        UPDATE vendors
        SET vend_state = v_vend_state
        WHERE vend_id = v_vend_id;
      END IF;

   -- When no more rows, exit
   EXIT WHEN c_vendors%notfound;

 END LOOP;

  -- Close cursor
  CLOSE c_vendors;

END;
```

Analysis ▼

This example is exactly the same as the prior example, until you get to the code within the `LOOP`. Previously we used `FETCH` to retrieve data and then did nothing with it. Here we've added some processing.

The `IF` statements checks to see whether the row that has been fetched is in the `USA`. If yes, it uses the `Upper()` function to convert the state (stored in variable `v_vend_state`) to uppercase.

Next, an `UPDATE` statement is used to update the vendors table with the corrected state, using variables both as the `SET` value and in the `WHERE` clause.

And then it's on to the next row.

To keep things simple, this example fixes one thing only—it makes sure that USA state abbreviations are in uppercase. In the real world, additional processing would be needed, and all sorts of rules could be provided, including additional `IF` blocks for other countries. In addition, this code is rather inefficient in that it updates the vendor unconditionally; if the state was already uppercase, then this `UPDATE` wouldn't be needed, and so a better implementation would only issue `UPDATE` statements if there were actually something to update. But you get the idea, and with this basic structure in place, it's easy to add extra programming logic and intelligence to the code.

> NOTE: `LOOP` **or** `REPEAT`**?**
>
> In addition to the `LOOP` statement used here, Oracle also supports a `REPEAT UNTIL` statement that can be used to repeat code (including cursors) until a condition is met. In general, you'll find the syntax of the `LOOP` statement makes it better suited for looping through cursors.

There you have it—a complete working example of cursors and row-by-row processing.

Summary

In this lesson, you learned what cursors are and why they are used. You also saw examples demonstrating basic cursor use, as well as techniques for looping through cursor results and for row-by-row processing.

LESSON 24

Using Triggers

In this lesson, you'll learn what triggers are, why they are used, and how. You'll also look at the syntax for creating and using them.

Understanding Triggers

Oracle statements are executed when needed, as are stored procedures. But what if you wanted a statement (or statements) to be executed automatically when events occur? For example:

- Every time a customer is added to a database table, check that the phone number is formatted correctly and that the state abbreviation is in uppercase.
- Every time a product is ordered, subtract the ordered quantity from the number in stock.
- Whenever a row is deleted, save a copy in an archive table.

What all these examples have in common is that they need to be processed automatically whenever an event occurs. That is exactly what triggers are. A *trigger* is an Oracle statement (or a group of statements enclosed within `BEGIN` and `END` statements) that are automatically executed by Oracle in response to any of these statements:

- `ALTER`
- `CREATE`
- `DROP`
- `DELETE`
- `INSERT`
- `UPDATE`

The last three are of the greatest interest—triggers that are executed in response to table row changes.

> NOTE: **Triggers on Database Operations**
>
> Oracle also supports triggers on server startup and shutdown, user login and logoff, and more. These are beyond the scope of this book, and are primarily of interest to database administrators.

Creating Triggers

When creating a trigger, you need to specify four pieces of information:

- The unique trigger name
- The table to which the trigger is to be associated
- The action that the trigger should respond to (`DELETE`, `INSERT`, or `UPDATE`)
- When the trigger should be executed (`BEFORE` or `AFTER` processing)

Triggers are created using the `CREATE TRIGGER` statement. Here is a simple example (which doesn't actually do anything useful, but does help explain the syntax needed):

Input ▼

```
CREATE OR REPLACE TRIGGER orders_after_insert
AFTER INSERT ON orders
FOR EACH ROW

BEGIN

END;
```

Analysis ▼

This example won't run; Oracle doesn't like code that does nothing, and if you try to execute it, an error is returned. That said, let's look at the code.

`CREATE OR REPLACE TRIGGER` is used to create the new trigger named `orders_after_insert`. Triggers can execute before or after an operation occurs, and here `AFTER INSERT ON` is specified so the trigger will execute after a successful `INSERT` statement has been executed. `INSERT` can insert multiple rows, and the trigger then specifies `FOR EACH ROW` and the code to be executed for each inserted row. So, whenever a product is added to the `customers` table, this trigger runs, and any code between `BEGIN` and `END` executes.

> NOTE: **When Triggers Fail**
>
> If a `BEFORE` trigger fails, Oracle does not perform the requested operation. In addition, if either a `BEFORE` trigger or the SQL statement itself fails, Oracle does not execute an `AFTER` trigger (if one exists).

Dropping Triggers

By now, the syntax for dropping a trigger should be self-apparent. To drop a trigger, use the `DROP TRIGGER` statement, as shown here:

Input ▼

```
DROP TRIGGER orders_after_insert;
```

Analysis ▼

To update a trigger, either `DROP` and then `CREATE` again, or use `CREATE OR REPLACE` as shown previously.

Using Triggers

With the basics covered, now look at each of the supported trigger types, and the differences between them.

`INSERT` Triggers

`INSERT` triggers execute `BEFORE` or `AFTER` an `INSERT` statement executes. Be aware of the following:

- Within `INSERT` trigger code, you can refer to a virtual table named `:NEW` to access the rows being inserted.
- In a `BEFORE INSERT` trigger, the values in `:NEW` may also be updated (allowing you to change values about to be inserted).

A common use for triggers is to track table changes (audit trails or logs). To try an example, you'll first need a table to store this information. This next Oracle SQL statement creates a table to store a log of all changes to the `orders` table:

Input ▼

```
CREATE TABLE orders_log
(
  changed_on  TIMESTAMP NOT NULL ,
  change_type CHAR(1)   NOT NULL ,
  order_num   INT       NOT NULL
);
```

Analysis ▼

This table has columns to store the change date and time, the type of change (`A` for added, `U` for updated, `D` for deleted), and the `order_num` of the order changed.

Now that you have a table to store the change log, you need to create the trigger that will update this new table. Here is the code:

Input ▼

```
CREATE OR REPLACE TRIGGER orders_after_insert
AFTER INSERT ON orders
FOR EACH ROW

BEGIN

  INSERT INTO orders_log(changed_on, change_type, order_num)
  VALUES(SYSDATE, 'A', :NEW.order_num);

END;
```

Analysis ▼

`CREATE OR REPLACE TRIGGER` is used to create the new trigger named `orders_after_insert`. Triggers can be executed before or after an operation occurs, and here `AFTER INSERT ON` is specified so the trigger will execute after a successful `INSERT` statement has been executed. The trigger then specifies `FOR EACH ROW` so that the trigger code will be executed for each row if `INSERT` inserts multiple rows. When a new order is saved in `orders`, Oracle executes the trigger, and inserts a new row into `orders_log`. The date and time is saved using `SYSTIME`, the action is set to `A` (for add), and the new number is obtained from `:NEW.order_num`.

The most important thing to note about this example is the use of the `:NEW` table. `:NEW` is not an actual table, but it can be used as one within triggers to access the new data. You'll see `:OLD` used the same way shortly.

To test this trigger, try inserting a new order, like this (feel free to change the values; just be sure to use a valid `cust_id`):

Input ▼

```
INSERT INTO orders(order_num, order_date, cust_id)
VALUES(20010, SYSDATE, 10001);
```

The `INSERT` statement itself does not return anything useful, but it did cause our trigger to be executed. To verify this, let's see what is in the `orders_log` table:

Input ▼

```
SELECT * FROM orders_log;
```

Output ▼

```
+--------------------+-------------+-----------+
| changed_on         | change_type | order_num |
+--------------------+-------------+-----------+
| 19-FEB-15 04.27.18 | A           |     20010 |
+--------------------+-------------+-----------+
```

Analysis ▼

orders_logs contains three columns. changed_on contains the date and time that the change occurred (returned by SYSDATE in the trigger), change_type is A (order added), and order_num contains the new order number.

> TIP: BEFORE **or** AFTER**?**
>
> This example used AFTER to execute the trigger after the new order was created. As a rule, use AFTER if you need to access data that won't exist until a statement has been processed. Use BEFORE for any data validation and cleanup (for example, if you want to make sure that the data inserted into the table was exactly as needed).

DELETE Triggers

DELETE triggers are executed before or after a DELETE statement is executed. Be aware of the following:

- Within DELETE trigger code, you can refer to a virtual table named :OLD to access the rows being deleted.
- The values in :OLD are all read-only and cannot be updated.

The following example demonstrates the use of :OLD to save rows about to be deleted into the log table:

Input ▼

```
CREATE OR REPLACE TRIGGER orders_before_delete
BEFORE DELETE ON orders
FOR EACH ROW

BEGIN

  INSERT INTO orders_log(changed_on, change_type, order_num)
  VALUES(SYSDATE, 'D', :OLD.order_num);

END;
```

Analysis ▼

This trigger is similar to the `orders_after_insert` trigger, but this one logs order deletions. This trigger is executed `BEFORE DELETE` (or you would not have access to the `order_num`).

If you were to delete the order you just inserted, you would see a second row in the `orders_log` table reflecting the deletion.

Another good use for `DELETE` triggers is to archive deletions (rows deleted from a table will automatically be saved in their entirety to an archive table). This updated version of the `orders_before_delete` trigger logs the deletion and also saves the deleted data to a table named `orders_archive` (you'll obviously need to create that table for this trigger to work; `orders_archive` will use the same `CREATE TABLE` statement as the one used to create `orders`):

Input ▼

```
CREATE OR REPLACE TRIGGER orders_before_delete
BEFORE DELETE ON orders
FOR EACH ROW

BEGIN

  -- Log deletion
  INSERT INTO orders_log(changed_on, change_type, order_num)
  VALUES(SYSDATE, 'D', :OLD.order_num);
  -- Archive it
  INSERT INTO orders_archive(order_num, order_date, cust_id)
  VALUES(:OLD.order_num, :OLD.order_date, :OLD.cust_id);
END;
```

Analysis ▼

Before any order is deleted, this trigger will be executed. In addition to the logging shown previously, this trigger uses an `INSERT` statement to save the values in `:OLD` (the order about to be deleted) into an archive table named `archive_orders`.

> TIP: **An Extra Level of Protection**
>
> The advantage of using a `BEFORE DELETE` trigger (as opposed to an `AFTER DELETE` trigger) is that if for some reason the order could not be archived, the `DELETE` itself will be aborted.

UPDATE Triggers

`UPDATE` triggers are executed before or after an `UPDATE` statement is executed. Be aware of the following:

- In `UPDATE` trigger code, you can refer to a virtual table named `:OLD` to access the previous (pre-`UPDATE` statement) values and `:NEW` to access the new updated values.
- In a `BEFORE UPDATE` trigger, the values in `:NEW` may also be updated (allowing you to change values about to be used in the `UPDATE` statement).
- The values in `:OLD` are all read-only and cannot be updated.

The following example ensures that state abbreviations are always in uppercase (regardless of how they were actually specified in the `UPDATE` statement):

Input ▼

```
CREATE OR REPLACE TRIGGER customers_before_update
BEFORE UPDATE ON customers
FOR EACH ROW

BEGIN

   :NEW.cust_state := Upper(:NEW.cust_state);

END;
```

Analysis ▼

Obviously, any data cleanup needs to occur in the `BEFORE UPDATE` statement as it does in this example. Each time a row is updated, the value in `:NEW.vend_state` (the value that will be used to update table rows) is replaced with `Upper(:NEW.vend_state)`. Notice that the trigger doesn't have to use an `UPDATE` statement to update the row. The trigger executes `BEFORE` the `UPDATE` is executed, and the code modifies the data in `:NEW` before it is used, so by the time Oracle executes the original `UPDATE` statement, the modified `cust_state` will be used.

Multi-Event Triggers

All the triggers we've seen thus far execute when a specific event (`INSERT`, `UPDATE`, or `DELETE`) occurs. Oracle allows triggers to be associated with multiple events. Here's an example, a minor modification to the last shown trigger:

Input ▼

```
CREATE OR REPLACE TRIGGER customers_before_update
BEFORE INSERT OR UPDATE ON customers
FOR EACH ROW

BEGIN

   :NEW.cust_state := Upper(:NEW.cust_state);

END;
```

Analysis ▼

The only change here is that `BEFORE UPDATE` has been changed to `BEFORE INSERT OR UPDATE`. This way our trigger, which forces correct case of `cust_state`, will be used for new customers as well as updates.

Of course, triggers that fire on multiple events must be compatible with all of those events. In our example, we used `:NEW`, which is indeed present for both `INSERT` and `UPDATE` operations, and so the trigger could safely be used for both events. Had our code used `:OLD`, which would be present for `UPDATE` but not `INSERT`, this reuse would not have been possible.

More on Triggers

Before wrapping this lesson, here are some important points to keep in mind when using triggers:

- Triggers are written in PL/SQL, and everything you've learned about PL/SQL thus far applies to triggers, too.
- Creating triggers might require special security access. However, trigger execution is automatic. If an `INSERT`, `UPDATE`, or `DELETE` statement might be executed, any associated triggers execute, too.
- Triggers should be used to ensure data consistency (case, formatting, and so on). The advantage of performing this type of processing in a trigger is that it always happens, and happens transparently, regardless of client application.
- One very interesting use for triggers is in creating an audit trail, as shown in this lesson. Using triggers, it would be easy to log changes (even before and after states if needed) to another table.
- Triggers can invoke other PL/SQL code, including functions and stored procedures.

Summary

In this lesson, you learned what triggers are and why they are used. You learned the trigger types and the times that they can be executed. You also saw examples of triggers used for `INSERT`, `DELETE`, and `UPDATE` operations.

LESSON 25

Managing Transaction Processing

In this lesson, you'll learn what transactions are and how to use `COMMIT` and `ROLLBACK` statements to manage transaction processing.

Understanding Transaction Processing

Transaction processing is used to maintain database integrity by ensuring that batches of Oracle SQL operations execute completely or not at all.

As explained back in Lesson 15, "Joining Tables," relational databases are designed so data is stored in multiple tables to facilitate easier data manipulation, management, and reuse. Without going in to the hows and whys of relational database design, take it as a given that well-designed database schemas are relational to some degree.

The orders tables you've been using in prior lessons are a good example of this. Orders are stored in two tables: `orders` stores actual orders, and `orderitems` stores the individual items ordered. These two tables are related to each other using unique IDs called primary keys (as discussed in Lesson 1, "Understanding SQL"). These tables, in turn, are related to other tables containing customer and product information.

The process of adding an order to the system is as follows:

1. Check whether the customer is already in the database (present in the `customers` table). If not, add him or her.

2. Retrieve the customer's ID.

3. Add a row to the `orders` table associating it with the customer ID.

4. Retrieve the new order ID assigned in the `orders` table.
5. Add one row to the `orderitems` table for each item ordered, associating it with the `orders` table by the retrieved ID (and with the `products` table by product ID).

Now imagine that some database failure (for example, out of disk space, security restrictions, table locks) prevents this entire sequence from completing. What would happen to your data?

Well, if the failure occurred after the customer was added and before the `orders` table was added, there is no real problem. It is perfectly valid to have customers without orders. When you run the sequence again, the inserted customer record will be retrieved and used. You can effectively pick up where you left off.

But what if the failure occurred after the `orders` row was added, but before the `orderitems` rows were added? Now you would have an empty order sitting in your database.

Worse, what if the system failed during adding the `orderitems` rows? Now you would end up with a partial order in your database, but you wouldn't know it.

How do you solve this problem? That's where *transaction processing* comes in. Transaction processing is a mechanism used to manage sets of SQL operations that must be executed in batches to ensure that databases never contain the results of partial operations. With transaction processing, you can ensure that sets of operations are not aborted mid-processing—they either execute in their entirety or not at all (unless explicitly instructed otherwise). If no error occurs, the entire set of statements is committed (written) to the database tables. If an error does occur, a rollback (undo) can occur to restore the database to a known and safe state.

So, looking at the same example, this is how the process would work:

1. Check whether the customer is already in the database; if not, add him or her.
2. Commit the customer information.
3. Retrieve the customer's ID.

4. Add a row to the `orders` table.

5. If a failure occurs while adding the row to `orders`, roll back.

6. Retrieve the new order ID assigned in the `orders` table.

7. Add one row to the `orderitems` table for each item ordered.

8. If a failure occurs while adding rows to `orderitems`, roll back all the `orderitems` rows added and the `orders` row.

9. Commit the order information.

When you're working with transactions and transaction processing, there are a few keywords that'll keep reappearing. Here are the terms you need to know:

- **Transaction**—A block of SQL statements
- **Rollback**—The process of undoing specified SQL statements
- **Commit**—Writing unsaved SQL statements to the database tables
- **Savepoint**—A temporary placeholder in a transaction set to which you can issue a rollback (as opposed to rolling back an entire transaction)

Controlling Transactions

Now that you know what transaction processing is, let's look at what is involved in managing transactions.

The key to managing transactions involves breaking your SQL statements into logical chunks and explicitly stating when data should be rolled back and when it should not.

Unlike most DBMSs, Oracle does not require you to start a transaction. In Oracle, transactions are implicit. Any time you execute a SQL statement, a transaction is started and finished, and if multiple, the statements are executed at once; all are contained within a single transaction.

Using ROLLBACK

The Oracle `ROLLBACK` command is used to roll back (undo) PL/SQL statements, as shown in this next statement:

Input ▼

```
SELECT * FROM orders_log;
DELETE FROM orders_log;
SELECT * FROM orders_log;
ROLLBACK;
SELECT * FROM orders_log;
```

Analysis ▼

This example starts by displaying the contents of the `orders_logs` table (this table was created in Lesson 24, "Using Triggers"). First a `SELECT` is performed to show that the table is not empty, and then all the rows are deleted with a `DELETE` statement. Another `SELECT` verifies that, indeed, `orders_logs` is empty. A `ROLLBACK` statement is then used to roll back all statements, and the final `SELECT` shows that the table is no longer empty.

Using COMMIT

Oracle SQL statements are usually executed and written directly to the database tables. This is known as an *implicit commit*—the commit (write or save) operation happens automatically.

In a transaction block, however, you might want to force an explicit commit so that data is saved by using the `COMMIT` statement, as shown here:

Input ▼

```
DELETE FROM orderitems WHERE order_num = 20010;
DELETE FROM orders WHERE order_num = 20010;
COMMIT;
```

Analysis ▼

In this example, order number `20010` is deleted entirely from the system. Because this involves updating two database tables, `orders` and `orderitems`, a transaction block is used to ensure that the order is not partially deleted. The final `COMMIT` statement writes the change only if no error occurred. If the first `DELETE` worked, but the second failed, the `DELETE` would not be committed (it would effectively be automatically undone).

The truth is that this example is not overly useful. If the first `DELETE` had failed, the transaction would have been terminated anyway and no implicit commit would have occurred. But imagine additional processing after the `COMMIT`, maybe updating stock quantities, or logging changes. The ability to control when commits occur then becomes important.

> NOTE: **Implicit Transaction Closes**
>
> After a `COMMIT` or `ROLLBACK` statement has been executed, the transaction is automatically closed (and future changes will implicitly commit).

Using Savepoints

Simple `ROLLBACK` and `COMMIT` statements enable you to write or undo an entire transaction. Although this works for simple transactions, more complex transactions might require partial commits or rollbacks.

For example, the process of adding an order described previously is a single transaction. If an error occurs, you only want to roll back to the point before the `orders` row was added. You do not want to roll back the addition to the `customers` table (if there was one).

To support the rollback of partial transactions, you must be able to put bookmarks at strategic locations in the transaction block. Then, if a rollback is required, you can roll back to one of the placeholders.

These bookmarks are called *savepoints*, and to create one, use the `SAVEPOINT` statement, as follows:

Input ▼

```
SAVEPOINT delete1;
```

Each savepoint takes a unique name that identifies it so that, when you roll back, Oracle knows where you are rolling back to. To roll back to this savepoint, do the following:

Input ▼

```
ROLLBACK TO SAVEPOINT delete1;
```

> TIP: **The More Savepoints the Better**
>
> You can have as many savepoints as you want in your Oracle SQL code, and the more the better. Why? Because the more savepoints you have, the more flexibility you have in managing rollbacks exactly as you need them.

Summary

In this lesson, you learned that transactions are blocks of SQL statements that must be executed as a batch. You learned how to use the `COMMIT` and `ROLLBACK` statements to explicitly manage when data is written and when it is undone. You also learned how to use savepoints to provide a greater level of control over rollback operations.

LESSON 26
Managing Security

Database servers usually contain critical data, and ensuring the safety and integrity of that data requires that access control be used. In this lesson, you'll learn about Oracle access control and user management.

Understanding Access Control

The basis of security for your Oracle server is this: *Users should have appropriate access to the data they need—no more and no less*. In other words, users should not have too much access to too much data.

Consider the following:

- Most users need to read and write data from tables, but few users will ever need to be able to create and drop tables.
- Some users might need to read tables but might not need to update them.
- You might want to allow users to add data, but not delete data.
- Some users (managers or administrators) might need rights to manipulate user accounts, but most should not.
- You might want users to access data via stored procedures, but never directly.
- You might want to restrict access to some functionality based on from where the user is logging in.

These are just examples, but they help demonstrate an important point. You need to provide users with the access they need and just the access they need. This is known as *access control*, and managing access control requires creating and managing user accounts.

Back in Lesson 3, "Working with Oracle," you learned that you need to log in to Oracle to perform any operations. When first installed, Oracle creates a user account named `SYSTEM` that has complete and total control over the entire Oracle server. You might have been using the `SYSTEM` login throughout the lessons in this book, and that is okay when experimenting with Oracle on non-live servers. But in the real world, you would never use `SYSTEM` on a day-to-day basis. Instead, you would create a series of accounts, some for administration, some for users, some for developers, and so on.

> NOTE: **Preventing Innocent Mistakes**
>
> It is important to note that access control is not just intended to keep out users with malicious intent. More often than not, data nightmares are the result of an inadvertent mistake, a mistyped Oracle statement, being in the wrong database, or some other user error. Access control helps avoid these situations by ensuring that users are unable to execute statements they should not be executing.

> CAUTION: **Don't Use** `SYSTEM`
>
> The `SYSTEM` login (actually, all the `SYS` logins—there might be multiple that start with `SYS`) should be considered sacred. Use it only when absolutely needed (perhaps if you cannot get into other administrative accounts). `SYSTEM` should never be used in day-to-day Oracle operations.

Managing Users

Oracle user accounts and information are stored in an Oracle database named `dba_users`. You usually do not need to access the `dba_users` table directly (most database administrators use client tools to manage accounts), but sometimes you might. One of those times is when you want to obtain a list of all user accounts. To do that, use the following code:

Input ▼

```
SELECT * FROM dba_users;
```

Analysis ▼

This SELECT statement lists all the defined users (and you'll be surprised by how many default accounts there). You'll also see account creation dates, last login time, and more.

Creating User Accounts

To create a new user account, use the CREATE USER statement, as shown here:

Input ▼

```
CREATE USER ben IDENTIFIED BY "p@$$w0rd";
```

Analysis ▼

CREATE USER creates a new user account. A password need not be specified at user account creation time, but this example does specify a password using IDENTIFIED BY "p@$$w0rd" (double quotes are needed; single quotes won't work).

If you were to list the user accounts again, you would see the new account listed in the output.

Deleting User Accounts

To delete a user account (along with any associated rights and privileges), use the DROP USER statement as shown here:

Input ▼

```
DROP USER ben;
```

> NOTE: **No Renaming**
>
> Oracle doesn't allow users to be renamed. If you need to rename a user, you'll need to DROP and CREATE again.

Setting Access Rights

With user accounts created, you must next assign access rights and privileges. Newly created user accounts have no access at all. They can log in to Oracle but will see no data and will be unable to perform any database operations.

Rights grants are referred to as *privileges*, and they are stored in the `sys.dba_sys_privs` table:

Input ▼

```
SELECT PRIVILEGE
FROM sys.dba_sys_privs
WHERE grantee = 'ben';
```

Analysis ▼

Because no privileges have been defined, this statement will return rows. Try it again for user `SYSTEM` and you'll see that everything is allowed.

To set rights, the `GRANT` statement is used. At a minimum, `GRANT` requires that you specify:

- The privilege being granted
- The item being granted access to
- The user name

The following example demonstrates the use of `GRANT`:

Input ▼

```
GRANT SELECT ON customers TO ben;
```

Analysis ▼

This `GRANT` allows the use of `SELECT` on `customers`. By granting `SELECT` access only, user `ben` has read-only access to the table.

Multiple grants may be specified at once:

Input ▼

```
GRANT SELECT, INSERT, UPDATE ON customers TO ben;
```

Analysis ▼

This GRANT allows the use of SELECT, INSERT, and UPDATE on table customers. So user ben would not be able to DELETE rows, and definitely not ALTER or DROP the table.

> TIP: **Use PL/SQL**
>
> You can use PL/SQL to create loops to batch the assigning of privileges. Of course, you could create stored procedures to do this, too.

The opposite of GRANT is REVOKE, which is used to revoke specific rights and permissions. Here is an example:

Input ▼

```
REVOKE INSERT, UPDATE, DELETE ON customers FROM ben;
```

Analysis ▼

Here GRANT TO is replaced with REVOKE FROM. This REVOKE statement takes away access granted to user ben. The access being revoked must exist or an error will be thrown.

Table 26.1 lists each of the table-level rights and privileges that may be granted or revoked. Table 26.2 lists some of the other important database rights and privileges; these privileges are usually tied to specific objects or can be used with ANY.

TABLE 26.1 Table Rights and Privileges

Privilege	Description
ALL	All privileges
ALTER	Use of ALTER TABLE

DELETE	Use of DELETE
INDEX	Use of CREATE INDEX and DROP INDEX
INSERT	Use of INSERT
REFERENCES	Use to create constraints
SELECT	Use of SELECT
UPDATE	Use of UPDATE

TABLE 26.2 Database Rights and Privileges

Privilege	Description
CREATE	Create database objects
ALTER	Alter database objects
DROP	Drop database objects
EXECUTE	Invoke methods

Using GRANT and REVOKE in conjunction with the privileges listed in Tables 26.1 and 26.2, you have complete control over what users can and cannot do with your precious data.

Changing Passwords

To change user passwords, use the ALTER USER statement, as shown here:

Input ▼

```
ALTER USER ben IDENTIFIED BY "l0ngerp@$$w0rd" REPLACE
➥"p@$$w0rd";
```

Summary

In this lesson, you learned about access control and how to secure your Oracle server by assigning specific rights to users. As you can imagine, there is a lot more to this advanced topic, and Oracle administrators should dedicate the time to fully understand managing DBMS security.

APPENDIX A
The Example Tables

Writing SQL statements requires a good understanding of the underlying database design. Without knowing what information is stored in what table, how tables are related to each other, and the actual breakup of data within a row, it is impossible to write effective SQL.

You are strongly advised to actually try every example in every lesson in this book. All the lessons use a common set of data files. To assist you in better understanding the examples and to enable you to follow along with the lessons, this appendix describes the tables used, their relationships, and how to obtain them.

Understanding the Sample Tables

The tables used throughout this book are part of an order entry system used by an imaginary distributor of paraphernalia that might be needed by your favorite cartoon characters (yes, cartoon characters; no one said that learning Oracle needed to be boring). The tables are used to perform several tasks, including:

- Manage vendors
- Manage product catalogs
- Manage customer lists
- Enter customer orders

Making this all work requires six tables that are closely interconnected as part of a relational database design. A description of each of the tables appears in the following sections.

> NOTE: **Simplified Examples**
>
> The tables used here are by no means complete. A real-world order entry system would have to keep track of lots of other data that has not been included here (for example, payment and accounting information, shipment tracking, and more). However, these tables do demonstrate the kinds of data organization and relationships you will encounter in most real installations. You can apply these techniques and technologies to your own databases.

What follows is a description of each of the six tables, along with the name of the columns within each table and their descriptions.

> NOTE: **Why Out of Order?**
>
> If you are wondering why the six tables are listed in the order they are, it is due to their dependencies. Because the `products` tables is dependent on the `vendors` table, `vendors` is listed first, and so on.

The `vendors` Table

The `vendors` table stores the vendors whose products are sold (see Table A.1). Every vendor has a record in this table, and that vendor ID (the `vend_id`) column is used to match products with vendors.

TABLE A.1 `vendors` Table Columns

Column	Description
vend_id	Unique numeric vendor ID
vend_name	Vendor name
vend_address	Vendor address
vend_city	Vendor city
vend_state	Vendor state
vend_zip	Vendor ZIP Code
vend_country	Vendor country

- All tables should have primary keys defined. This table should use `vend_id` as its primary key. `vend_id` is an auto increment field.

The `products` Table

The `products` table contains the product catalog, one product per row (see Table A.2). Each product has a unique ID (the `prod_id` column) and is related to its vendor by `vend_id` (the vendor's unique ID).

TABLE A.2 `products` Table Columns

Column	Description
prod_id	Unique product ID
vend_id	Product vendor ID (relates to vend_id in vendors table)
prod_name	Product name
prod_price	Product price
prod_desc	Product description

- All tables should have primary keys defined. This table should use `prod_id` as its primary key.
- To enforce referential integrity, a foreign key should be defined on `vend_id`, relating it to `vend_id` in `vendors`.

The `customers` Table

The `customers` table stores all customer information (see Table A.3). Each customer has a unique ID (the `cust_id` column).

TABLE A.3 `customers` Table Columns

Column	Description
cust_id	Unique numeric customer ID
cust_name	Customer name
cust_address	Customer address
cust_city	Customer city

cust_state	Customer state
cust_zip	Customer ZIP Code
cust_country	Customer country
cust_contact	Customer contact name
cust_email	Customer contact email address

- All tables should have primary keys defined. This table should use cust_id as its primary key. cust_id is an auto increment field.

The orders Table

The orders table stores customer orders (but not order details), as shown in Table A.4. Each order is uniquely numbered (the order_num column). Orders are associated with the appropriate customers by the cust_id column (which relates to the customer's unique ID in the customers table).

TABLE A.4 orders Table Columns

Column	Description
order_num	Unique order number
order_date	Order date
cust_id	Order customer ID (relates to cust_id in customers table)

- All tables should have primary keys defined. This table should use order_num as its primary key. order_num is an auto increment field.
- To enforce referential integrity, a foreign key should be defined on cust_id, relating it to cust_id in customers.

The orderitems Table

The orderitems table stores the actual items in each order, one row per item per order (see Table A.5). For every row in orders, there are one or more rows in orderitems. Each order item is uniquely identified by the order number plus the order item (first item in order, second item in order, and so on). Order items are associated with their appropriate order by the `order_num` column (which relates to the order's unique ID in `orders`). In addition, each order item contains the product ID of the item orders (which relates the item back to the `products` table).

TABLE A.5 `orderitems` Table Columns

Column	Description
`order_num`	Order number (relates to `order_num` in `orders` table)
`order_item`	Order item number (sequential within an order)
`prod_id`	Product ID (relates to `prod_id` in `products` table)
`quantity`	Item quantity
`item_price`	Item price

- All tables should have primary keys defined. This table should use `order_num` and `order_item` as its primary keys.
- To enforce referential integrity, foreign keys should be defined on `order_num`, relating it to `order_num` in `orders`, and `prod_id`, relating it to `prod_id` in `products`.

The `productnotes` Table

The `productnotes` table stores notes associated with specific products (see Table A.6). Not all products may have associated notes, and some products may have many associated notes.

TABLE A.6 `productnotes` Table Columns

Column	Description
`note_id`	Unique note id
`prod_id`	Product ID (corresponds to `prod_id` in `products` table)
`note_date`	Date note added
`note_text`	Note text

- All tables should have primary keys defined. This table should use note_id as its primary key.
- To enforce referential integrity, a foreign key should be defined on prod_id, relating it to prod_id in products.

APPENDIX B

Oracle PL/SQL Datatypes

As explained in Lesson 1, "Understanding SQL," datatypes are basically rules that define what data may be stored in a column and how that data is actually stored.

Datatypes are used for several reasons:

- Datatypes enable you to restrict the type of data that can be stored in a column. For example, a numeric datatype column only accepts numeric values.
- Datatypes allow for more efficient storage, internally. Numbers and date time values can be stored in a more condensed format than text strings.
- Datatypes allow for alternate sorting orders. If everything is treated as strings, `1` comes before `10`, which comes before `2`. (Strings are sorted in dictionary sequence, one character at a time starting from the left.) As numeric datatypes, the numbers would be sorted correctly.

When designing tables, pay careful attention to the datatypes being used. Using the wrong datatype can seriously impact your application. Changing the datatypes of existing populated columns is not a trivial task. (In addition, doing so can result in data loss.)

Although this appendix is by no means a complete tutorial on datatypes and how they are to be used, it explains the major Oracle datatype types, and what they are used for.

String Datatypes

The most commonly used datatypes are string datatypes. These store strings: for example, names, addresses, phone numbers, and ZIP Codes. As listed in Table B.1, there are basically two types of string datatype that you can use—fixed-length strings and variable-length strings.

Fixed-length strings are datatypes that are defined to accept a fixed number of characters, and that number is specified when the table is created. For example, you might allow 30 characters in a first-name column or 11 characters in a Social Security Number column (the exact number needed allowing for the two dashes). Fixed-length columns do not allow more than the specified number of characters. They also allocate storage space for as many characters as specified. So, if the string `Ben` is stored in a 30-character first-name field, a full 30 bytes are stored. `CHAR` is an example of a fixed-length string type.

Variable-length strings store text of variable length. Some variable-length datatypes have a defined maximum size. Others are entirely variable. Either way, only the data specified is saved (and no extra data is stored). `VARCHAR` is an example of a variable-length string type.

If variable-length datatypes are so flexible, why would you ever want to use fixed-length datatypes? The answer is performance. Oracle can sort and manipulate fixed-length columns far more quickly than it can sort variable-length columns. In addition, Oracle does not allow you to index variable-length columns (or the variable portion of a column). This also dramatically affects performance.

TABLE B.1 String Datatypes

Datatype	Description
`CHAR`	Fixed-length string from 1 to 2,000 characters long. Its size must be specified at create time.
`LOB`	Variable-length text with a maximum size of 8TB.
`LONG`	Same as `LOB`, but with a maximum size of 2GB. Use of `LONG` is no longer recommended, and `LOB` should be used instead.
`NCHAR`	Same as `CHAR`, but supports Unicode text.

NVARCHAR	Same as VARCHAR, but supports Unicode text.
VARCHAR	Variable-length text with a maximum size of 4,000 characters.

TIP: **Using Quotes**

Regardless of the form of string datatype being used, string values must always be surrounded by quotes (single quotes are often preferred).

CAUTION: **When Numeric Values Are Not Numeric Values**

You might think that phone numbers and ZIP Codes should be stored in numeric fields (after all, they only store numeric data), but doing so would not be advisable. If you store the ZIP Code 01234 in a numeric field, the number 1234 would be saved. You would actually lose a digit.

The basic rule to follow is: If the number is used in calculations (sums, averages, and so on), it belongs in a numeric datatype column. If it is used as a literal string (that happens to contain only digits), it belongs in a string datatype column.

Numeric Datatypes

Numeric datatypes store numbers. Unlike most DBMSs, Oracle really supports one major numeric type that supports both fixed- and floating-point numbers. Table B.2 lists the Oracle numeric datatypes.

TABLE B.2 Numeric Datatypes

Datatype	Description
BINARY_FLOAT	Floating-point value with 32-bit precision.
BINARY_DOUBLE	Floating-point value with 64-bit precision.
NUMBER	Positive and negative whole numbers, and floating-point numbers with up to 38 digits of precision. Can also be referred to as INT, INTEGER, DECIMAL, or NUMERIC.

> TIP: **Not Using Quotes**
>
> Unlike strings, numeric values should never be enclosed within quotes.

> TIP: **Storing Currency**
>
> There is no special Oracle datatype for currency values; use `NUMBER(8,2)` instead.

Date and Time Datatypes

Oracle uses special datatypes for the storage of date and time values, as listed in Table B.3.

TABLE B.3 Date and Time Datatypes

Datatype	Description
`DATE`	Date, but not time.
`TIMESTAMP`	Date and time.
`TIMESTAMP WITH TIME ZONE`	Date and time with time zone support.

Binary Datatypes

Binary datatypes are used to store all sorts of data (even binary information), such as graphic images, multimedia, and word processor documents (see Table B.4).

TABLE B.4 Binary Datatypes

Datatype	Description
`BLOB`	Unstructured binary data with a maximum length of 128TB.
`BFILE`	Data stored in an external file.
`CLOB`	Text with a maximum length of 128TB.

> NOTE: **Datatypes in Use**
>
> If you would like to see a real-world example of how different databases are used, see the sample table creation scripts (described in Appendix A, "The Example Tables").

APPENDIX C

Oracle PL/SQL Reserved Words and Keywords

Oracle PL/SQL is made up of *keywords*—special words that are used in performing SQL operations. Special care must be taken to not use these keywords when naming databases, tables, columns, and any other database objects.

ALL	END	OPTION
ALTER	EXCEPTION	OR
AND	EXCLUSIVE	ORDER,OVERLAPS
ANY	EXISTS	PRIOR
ARRAY	FETCH	PROCEDURE
ARROW	FOR	PUBLIC
AS	FORM	RANGE
ASC	FROM	RECORD
AT	GOTO	RESOURCE
BEGIN	GRANT	REVOKE
BETWEEN	GROUP	SELECT
BY	HAVING	SHARE
CASE	IDENTIFIED	SIZE
CHECK	IF	SQL
CLUSTER	IN	START
CLUSTERS	INDEX	SUBTYPE
COLAUTH	INDEXES	TABAUTH
COLUMNS	INSERT	TABLE
COMPRESS	INTERSECT	THEN
CONNECT	INTO	TO
CRASH	IS	TYPE
CREATE	LIKE	UNION
CURRENT	LOCK	UNIQUE
DECIMAL	MINUS	UPDATE
DECLARE	MODE	USE
DEFAULT	NOCOMPRESS	VALUES
DELETE	NOT	VIEW
DESC	NOWAIT	VIEWS
DISTINCT	NULL	WHEN
DROP	OF	WHERE
ELSE	ON	WITH

In addition to the Oracle PL/SQL reserved words, the following list of words (while legal to use) have special meaning to Oracle, and their use is not recommended.

A	DATA	LEADING
ADD	DATE	LENGTH
AGENT	DATE_BASE	LEVEL
AGGREGATE	DAY	LIBRARY
ARRAY	DEFINE	LIKE2
ATTRIBUTE	DETERMINISTIC	LIKE4
AUTHID	DOUBLE	LIKEC
AVG	DURATION	LIMIT
BFILE_BASE	ELEMENT	LIMITED
BINARY	ELSIF	LOCAL
BLOB_BASE	EMPTY	LONG
BLOCK	ESCAPE	LOOP
BODY	EXCEPT	MAP
BOTH	EXCEPTIONS	MAX
BOUND	EXECUTE	MAXLEN
BULK	EXIT	MEMBER
BYTE	EXTERNAL	MERGE
C	FINAL	MIN
CALL	FIXED	MINUTE
CALLING	FLOAT	MOD
CASCADE	FORALL	MODIFY
CHAR	FORCE	MONTH
CHAR_BASE	FUNCTION	MULTISET
CHARACTER	GENERAL	NAME
CHARSET	HASH	NAN
CHARSETFORM	HEAP	NATIONAL
CHARSETID	HIDDEN	NATIVE
CLOB_BASE	HOUR	NCHAR
CLOSE	IMMEDIATE	NEW
COLLECT	INCLUDING	NOCOPY
COMMENT	INDICATOR	NUMBER_BASE
COMMIT	INDICES	OBJECT
COMMITTED	INFINITE	OCICOLL
COMPILED	INSTANTIABLE	OCIDATE
CONSTANT	INT	OCIDATETIME
CONSTRUCTOR	INTERFACE	OCIDURATION
CONTEXT	INTERVAL	OCIINTERVAL
CONVERT	INVALIDATE	OCILOBLOCATOR
COUNT	ISOLATION	OCINUMBER
CURSOR	JAVA	OCIRAW
CUSTOMDATUM	LANGUAGE	OCIREF
DANGLING	LARGE	OCIREFCURSOR

OCIROWID
OCISTRING
OCITYPE
ONLY
OPAQUE
OPEN
OPERATOR
ORACLE
ORADATA
ORGANIZATION
ORLANY
ORLVARY
OTHERS
OUT
OVERRIDING
PACKAGE
PARALLEL_ENABLE
PARAMETER
PARAMETERS
PARTITION
PASCAL
PIPE
PIPELINED
PRAGMA
PRECISION
PRIVATE
RAISE
RANGE
RAW
READ
RECORD
REF
REFERENCE
REM
REMAINDER
RENAME
RESULT
RETURN
RETURNING
REVERSE
ROLLBACK
ROW
SAMPLE
SAVE
SAVEPOINT
SB1
SB2
SB4
SECOND
SEGMENT
SELF
SEPARATE
SEQUENCE
SERIALIZABLE
SET
SHORT
SIZE_T
SOME
SPARSE
SQLCODE
SQLDATA
SQLNAME
SQLSTATE
STANDARD
STATIC
STDDEV
STORED
STRING
STRUCT
STYLE
SUBMULTISET
SUBPARTITION
SUBSTITUTABLE
SUBTYPE
SUM
SYNONYM
TDO
THE
TIME
TIMESTAMP
TIMEZONE_ABBR
TIMEZONE_HOUR
TIMEZONE_MINUTE
TIMEZONE_REGION
TRAILING
TRANSAC
TRANSACTIONAL
TRUSTED
TYPE
UB1
UB2
UB4
UNDER
UNSIGNED
UNTRUSTED
USE
USING
VALIST
VALUE
VARIABLE
VARIANCE
VARRAY
VARYING
VOID
WHILE
WORK
WRAPPED
WRITE
YEAR
ZONE

Index

Symbols

A

B

C

D

E

F

J

K

L

M

N

O

R

T

U

V

W–X–Y–Z